The Second Chance Revolution: Becoming Your Own Boss After 50

Edward G. Rogoff, Ph.D.

and

David L. Carroll

Foreword by
Harry R. Moody, Ph.D.
Director of Academic Affairs, AARP

Copyrighted Material

The Second Chance Revolution: Becoming Your Own Boss After 50
Copyright © 2009 by Rowhouse Publishing

ALL RIGHTS RESERVED

No part of this publication may be reproduced, stored in a retrieval system or transmitted, in any form or by any means—electronic, mechanical, photocopying, recording or otherwise—without prior written permission, except for the inclusion of brief quotations in a review.

For information about this title or to order other books and/or electronic media, contact the publisher:

Rowhouse Publishing
1375 Broadway, Suite 600
New York, NY 10018
(877) 363-9866

info@rowhousepublishing.com
www.rowhousepublishing.com

Library of Congress Control Number: 2009906869

ISBN: 978-0-9791522-9-0

Printed in Canada

Cover design by David Grillo
Book design by 1106 Design

Publisher's Cataloging-In-Publication Data

    Rogoff, Edward G., 1951–

        The second chance revolution : becoming your own boss after 50 / Edward G. Rogoff and David L. Carroll ; foreword by Harry R. Moody. — 1st ed. New York : Rowhouse Pub., c2009.

        p. ; cm.

        ISBN: 978-0-9791522-9-0
        Includes bibliographical references and index.

        1. Career changes. 2. Entrepreneurship. 3. Vocational guidance. 4. Self-actualization (Psychology) I. Carroll, David, 1942– II. Title.

HF5384 .R64 2009	2009906869
650.1/4—dc22	0910

Table of Contents

Acknowledgments v

Foreword vii

Chapter 1: If You Come to a Fork in the Career Road, Take It! . . . 1

Chapter 2: Choosing an Entrepreneurial Profession That's Right for You 25

Chapter 3: On the Money: Conventional and Not-So-Conventional Ways to Finance a Business After Fifty 53

Chapter 4: What Every Entrepreneur Hates: Legal Issues, Boards of Directors, Insurance, and Taxes 73

Chapter 5: Your Personal Work-at-Home Handbook 91

Chapter 6: Networking for Building a Solid New Business 117

Chapter 7: The Franchise 127

Chapter 8: Fifty-Plus Business—Plus Family 157

Chapter 9: Why Build When You Can Purchase? The Ins and Outs of Buying an Existing Business 169

Index 179

Acknowledgments

This book is very much the product of our interaction with entrepreneurs, experts, and the people who have helped create the environment in which we work and learn. Author Edward Rogoff, as a professor at Baruch College, Chair of its Management Department, and former Director of the Lawrence N. Field Center for Entrepreneurship, has benefited from an extraordinary group of academic colleagues, including: Ramona Zachary, Alvin Puryear, Thomas Lyons, Micki Eisenman, Robert Foskey, Elissa Grossman, and Myung-Soo Lee. These fine people have been teachers, friends, and co-authors at various times. Bob Wolf of FJC Foundation is the person who started me and the team at Baruch down the path of examining the phenomenon of later life entrepreneurship. Bob is a brilliant thinker on this and many other topics. Author David Carroll, drawing on his many years as a self-help expert and author, made many of the contacts that make this book stand out.

Most importantly, Baruch College has been able to become a standout in the field of entrepreneurship studies because of the leadership, support, and generosity of Mr. Lawrence N. Field, a successful entrepreneur who built a real estate business through hard work, smart strategy, and strong ethics. He returned to his alma mater to create an environment that would help others do what he had done. And he has far exceeded his goal. Today, Baruch is not just a top school in entrepreneurship, but its entrepreneurship program is the largest in the nation.

At the Field Center, a superior staff has created a system that allowed us to interface with literally thousands of entrepreneurs, and learn from them. The staff at the Field Center includes Monica Dean, Ulas Neftci, Lendynette Pacheco, Jim Daley, Alyce Mayo, and Shaiu-Larn Hoang. We have also had the privilege of working with many fine entrepreneurs. High on the list of those whose knowledge and wisdom have found their way into *The Second Chance Revolution* are Michael Corbett (with whom Ed co-authored *The Entrepreneurial Conversation*) and David Roth of Get Stirred Up, an innovation-focused consultancy.

We interviewed many people for this book, and their stories are used as examples. Some people preferred not to have their names used, lest their candor interfere with their businesses or, perhaps, be seen as criticism of their partners or business associates. In such cases, of course, we used fictitious names for the entrepreneur and his or her business.

Among the people whose names are their own are Martha Zach, Joseph Gooden, Leslie Krasner, Paula Hornbeck, Kurt Thometz, Anne Homes, Darrel Skates, Ram Bahadur, Maxine Martens, John Lamie, Gene Wayne, Alan Winter, Jim Lorenzen, and Tom Klein.

We can't thank these men and women enough for helping us, but more importantly, for helping you, the reader, to witness examples of how entrepreneurship after 50 can help you to find the meaning in the workplace that has so long evaded you, and in the process revolutionize your life.

Foreword

by Harry R. Moody, Ph.D.
Director of Academic Affairs, AARP

People come to entrepreneurship in later life by many roads. Think of what Shakespeare said about greatness: "Some are born great, some achieve greatness and some have greatness thrust upon them."

The same could be said about entrepreneurship.

We all know people who are "born entrepreneurs" from childhood: that girl with the lemonade stand at the end of the block, that guy hawking class rings and mugs. Still others achieve entrepreneurial skills as they move through life. Think of those who spend their lives dreaming about running a sky lodge or a restaurant. They wonder: is it too late for me? Some achieve the skills and live out the dream.

Finally, in today's downbeat economy, there are men and women who have entrepreneurship thrust upon them. The reasons for this are many: downsizing, age-discrimination, loss of pension assets and jobs. Among aging boomers today, an alarm bell has gone off: It is no longer the age of your grandfather's Oldsmobile (or retirement). Today growing numbers of people over 50 expect to work much longer into what were once thought of as the retirement years. If assets and home equity are down, work-life extension is the only solution. But where will they find the jobs?

The answer is, in many cases, they will create these jobs *themselves* through their own initiative, talent, and perseverance. Which brings us back to self-employment and entrepreneurship again.

The United States may be on the cusp of an entrepreneurship boom because of its aging population. As it turns out, the baby boom that followed World War II is becoming the entrepreneurship boom of the twenty-first century. In the past decade, 55- to 64-year-olds were more likely to start their own companies than any other age group, according to research by the Kauffman Foundation. The average age of technology firm founders in the United States is 39, with twice as many over 50 as under 25.

What you will find by reading this book is that later-life entrepreneurship is not one adventure, but many. Or said another way, not one story but many stories. It could be a story in which your last chapter is your best chapter, a time for becoming your own boss, or, better, "becoming the person you were meant to be."

Theologian Frederick Buechner put it this way: "Your vocation is the place where your deep gladness meets the world's great hunger."

Still, once we decide on self-employment, troubling questions remain. Can I create a business that truly reflects the person I was meant to be? Is it too late to be on my own? Can I take the risk?

This book cannot answer those questions because each of us must find the courage to take the leap and find our own way. This book *can* give vital help to those who are getting ready to make the great leap.

The fact is that others have gone before us, and the great message of this book is: "It's not too late." Whether entrepreneurship is born, or achieved, or thrust upon us, it is not too late if we learn the skills necessary to make the journey. In this book, Professor Edward Rogoff and author David Carroll have put together the indispensable tools needed to make that journey and, finally, to find the deep gladness that comes from successful entrepreneurship in later life.

                    Harry R. Moody, Ph.D.
                    Director of Academic Affairs, AARP

Chapter 1
If You Come to a Fork in the Career Road, Take It!

From lemons to lemonade stand

"I stumbled out of my manager's office into the very long, all-of-a-sudden-too-brightly lit corridor," Frank Denton told me over lunch not so long ago.

Frank's a large jovial man in his mid-fifties, and a banker by profession. "My legs were unsteady, rubbery. You know that feeling. I was wondering if I was going to make it to the water cooler."

During my years as a professor of entrepreneurship at Baruch College in New York City, I had often come to Frank for advice when banking technicalities came up in my courses. We hadn't talked for some time, and there was much catching up to do.

"I'd seen it coming for a while," he told me, pulling at his collar à la Rodney Dangerfield. "People were getting laid off right and left at a lot of our branches. But you know, you think you're bulletproof. It's never going to happen to *me*. When my boss waved the pink slip under my nose, I was floored!"

Hearing Frank's distressing and all-too-common story I began to sympathize: Must be rough to lose a longtime job in your mid-fifties. It's so scary out there in the cold world. Blah blah, blah. Before I got off too many more commiserating clichés, he cut me short.

"Actually, Ed, losing my job was the best thing that could have ever happened!"

"Really! Why?"

"Because I was never all that happy working at the bank. It was okay, you know, just a job. But my number-one interest has always been stamps. Ever since I was a kid."

"Stamps?" I asked. "As in *stamp* collecting?"

"Yep. The kids used to call me 'George' in school 'cause I brought in so many of those two and three cent George Washington stamps for class projects. I love that stuff."

"Follow your bliss after fifty," I said.

"That's what I figured. It's now or never. Soooooo—after a few weeks at home recovering from layoff shock and realizing that I was a free man but also that time was marching on, it hit me. I was being handed the opportunity of a lifetime. How often do you get such a chance? I could now do what I'd always really *wanted* to do—for the rest of my life!"

Frank spoke the last sentence with exaggerated slowness, then paused to let the words sink in.

"And what was it exactly that I wanted to do? That was a no-brainer. I took part of my own collection of first-day covers and revenue stamps, hired a computer nerd to make me a website, put them up for sale, and presto! I'm an online stamp dealer."

"That's a fairly dramatic change of careers," I offered, sounding perhaps more surprised than I was. After all, I teach college courses on entrepreneurship every day at Baruch College, and I'm currently involved in several projects relating to independent business ventures after age fifty. Over the years, I've seen many people like Frank do a 180-degree turn in their professional lives when they reach the middle years. More times than not this turn leads in the direction of a person's real—and often long frustrated—dreams.

"Every career change is dramatic," Frank chuckled. "If any one knows that, it's you, Ed. Right? It's part of the fun."

It was true. At the Lawrence N. Field Center for Entrepreneurship at Baruch College, people Frank's age frequently describe their new business ventures using this same word: *fun*. I'm always a little taken aback when I hear it. "Fun," after all, makes you think of—what? Seeing a movie with friends? Hobnobbing at a party? Skiing? It's a term that doesn't come up a whole lot when people are talking about their longtime, day-to-day, nine-to-five job.

I asked Frank how he was doing.

"Right now, I'm handling a lot of quality stuff at a pretty good pace," he replied. "Sometimes my wife and I do weekend stamp markets. Auctions. I'm not making the salary I used to, of course. But I'm doing what I love and making enough to live decently."

He paused again then broke into a large grin. "And I'm sure a lot more relaxed than when I was talking to bank clients all day long on the telephone and shuffling through loan applications. I'm a happy man."

Join the Second Chance Revolution

Some call it a silent revolution, but this is a misnomer.

The new change in American work demographics is not silent at all. It is one of the most noted social phenomena of our day, its engine fuelled by the 77 million men and women born between 1946 and 1964—the famed baby boomer generation.

There are many interesting facts and figures that could be quoted about boomers getting older. You've already heard a number of them. The most significant for our purposes is this: A recent survey tells us that among men and women between the ages of fifty to seventy-five—an age cohort that is richly populated with boomers and that now accounts for more than a third of the labor pool in the United States—almost seventy percent plan *never* to retire.

Why?

Well, we'll get into the reasons for this decision in a minute. What's important to note here is that millions of older men and women in the United States are choosing to remain in the work force, people who up to a decade ago would have automatically taken their gold watch and retired when the age-sixty-five gong rang in their ears.

This new non-retirement trend is discussed on TV, over blogs, in best-selling books. It is talked over around office coffee machines, analyzed in sixtieth-floor executive suites, joked about on late-night talk programs, and hashed out in the back booths of a thousand after-hours watering holes. The subject is constantly on the lips of people who are approaching retirement age. More to the point, it is constantly in the back of their minds. Their concern is simple and urgent: Millions of fifty-plus Americans have highly honed job skills, a lifetime of vocational experience, and a broad array of talents at their chosen professions. They are also about to be, have recently been, or currently are unemployed.

Many of these people are anxious to become engaged in a business that will fill the gap between their retirement income and their current living needs. Others are eager to start a venture on their own that allows them to fulfill longtime professional dreams. These people are all members—or potential members—of the Second Chance Revolution.

Love, work, and other ways to survive

Why do so many men and women over the age of fifty wish to remain in the work force?

Two reasons: 1) They want to work; and 2) they need to work.

Want and need. That's it in a nutshell.

First, want. Keep in mind the fact that people over fifty are at the very summit of their powers. No other consolidation of wage earners in this country boasts such a rich treasure trove of expertise, confidence, and professional wisdom as the fifty-plus generation.

Most members of this age group, studies show, are better educated and healthier than were their counterparts of twenty or thirty years ago. Statistically speaking, they will live to a greater age than any generation in all recorded history. From the standpoint of opportunity, there are more job possibilities open to over-fifties now than at any time in our country's past.

As a result, a majority of people in this age bracket entertain no plans for retirement. Why should they? They're engaged and involved, and they want things to stay that way.

Here, lessons from the dictionary are revealing. One definition of retirement is to "go to bed." Another is to "recede," and another is to "take out of circulation." Still another is to "enter seclusion."

You get the point.

A relatively new concept, job retirement first saw the light of day immediately after the Civil War when army pensions from the government were pumping large sums of cash into the economy. This influx of largesse allowed veterans to spend their later years cutting back on their work hours and sometimes removing themselves from the work force entirely. At the same time, this abundance of money improved national income levels and personal standards of living as well.

The outcome of the marriage between leisure time and prosperity was that participation of persons sixty-five and older in the work force declined from seventy-eight percent in 1880 to less than twenty percent in 1990. In the process, an entirely new social ideal was born—rest at the end of life as a reward for a life of hard work.

Soon a new social equation followed: Retirement equals self-imposed inactivity. Somehow doing what you like came to mean doing nothing at all. In 1961, with his term as president nearing its close, a reporter asked Dwight D. Eisenhower what he intended to do when he left office. "I'm going to sit in my rocking chair," Ike replied. "And after the first six months I'm going to start thinking about rocking."

Since the great general's time, attitudes toward retirement have undergone a compelling transformation. Today, many people view the prospect of rocking away one's latter years as a kind of living death.

The notion of lifetime employment thus comes naturally to today's fifty-plus generation. In their minds, retirement is an obsolete notion—unnatural, absurd even. These work warriors want to stay relevant and employed. They also want to make their own rules of the game.

"What I do at retirement will be what I *want* to do, and *thrill* to do, and *yearn* to do, and *love* to do, and do so very, very well," a fifty-two-year-old photographer rhapsodized to me during one of my classes in later-life entrepreneurship.

"It's the time in life when I start to be whatever age I damn well please to be," another student told me. "I think I'm in my middle years," a sixty-five-year-old Bob Dylan once informed *Rolling Stone* magazine. "I have no plans to retire."

A survey conducted in 2006 by AARP reports that sixty-nine percent of people between forty-five and seventy-four are committed to staying employed as long as they possibly can. In another AARP study, sixty-eight percent of individuals between fifty and seventy intend to work in some capacity into their retirement years—or to never retire. Remaining involved and engrossed is clearly one of this age cohort's primary reasons for staying in the work force. Indeed, for many years, AARP itself was known as the American Association of

Retired Persons. Then, as the twenty-first century dawned, they made a command decision to change their name to AARP. No acronym now; the name was simply AARP. Why? Because AARP discovered that forty percent of its membership was still working.

> Since the middle of the nineteenth century, retirement in America has been viewed as a time of life when people withdraw to the quiet of their parlors, their hobbies—and their memories. Today, things work a bit differently; and as almost all surveys on the subject clearly show, most of us welcome the change. As the now somewhat shopworn phrase decrees, "Today, sixty has become the new forty."

Of course, there is also another reason why people of retirement age remain in the workplace. These people may or may not *want* to work, but they definitely *need* to work.

In an era dominated by creeping inflation, high health care costs, and a volatile financial market, few can afford to rest on their economic laurels. Traditional pensions and medical benefits have eroded and sometimes disappeared entirely. Costs of living are rising while salaries remain static. It is estimated that sixty to seventy percent of boomers who leave their jobs at retirement will have insufficient income to remain financially independent into their later years.

And there is also the psychological side to consider.

"For many people," insists famed writer and futurist, Alvin Toffler, "a job is crucial psychologically, over and above the paycheck. By making clear demands on their time and energy, it provides an element of structure around which the rest of their lives can be organized."

"To work is to pray" reads the motto of the Benedictine Order, and this saying might easily be adapted by many in today's fifty-plus generation for whom work is a kind of spiritual touch point—a way to stay connected with the rhythms of this busy world, with other people, with nature itself.

"Work is what I do," an aging friend once told me. "It's what they'll write about me on my tombstone."

In short, members of the fifty-plus generation want to keep working and/or need to keep working. Most love working. When asked about the meaning of life, Sigmund Freud gave an uncharacteristically

brief reply. "Love and work" was all he said, but his answer was wise. For a majority of people over fifty, these two essential human activities are linked.

This time around, however, for those in the fifty-plus zone there will be a major change of intention and perspective. The coming years, these people tell us, will be counted less as down time, and more as what *Washington Post* columnist, Abigail Trafford, describes as, "my time." The professional fulfillment that so long eluded them while in the employ of other people is now in their crosshairs, they tell us. Riding the wave of the Second Chance Revolution, they will now work at what they love and love what they work at.

What's more, while making this transition, many of these career warriors will make an extraordinary discovery. They will realize that the best years of their work life lie *ahead of them*, not behind.

They will find that, when equipped with the proper tools and the right information, the downward spiral of job loss, forced retirement, and ageism can be morphed into an entrepreneurial Yellow Brick Road. Millions of members of the fifty-plus generation can become—and want to become—their own bosses.

They want to become entrepreneurs.

Fielding your biggest questions

Since this is a book about "going entrepreneurial" in the second half of life, it is time for us to ask you a key question: Do you intend to keep working when retirement time comes around?

The answer, if you'll forgive the liberty, is most likely yes. Especially since you are reading this book. So, here's a second question: Are you tired of working for another person? Do you want to be your own boss?

Again, the answer probably is yes. Perhaps even definitely yes.

And that's good because the options for self-employment in the United States today are legion. They include owning your own business, investing in another's small business, independent contracting, consulting, franchising, participating in service professions, and many more possibilities, all of which we will look at carefully in the chapters that follow.

And, finally, the most important question: Is fifty-plus entrepreneurship a good idea for you in particular? Does it fit your specific needs, ambitions, and inclinations at this stage in your life?

Let's have a look.

Nay and yea

When the matter of future employment is raised among people over fifty, two voices compete for attention—let's call them Nay and Yea.

Nay likes to talk about things that are very scary. Nay likes to scare you.

Take Ralph as a case in point. Ralph is fifty-six. He's approaching retirement age. How does he intend to continue making a living after he leaves—or loses—his longtime job? Who is going to hire him when there is so much young blood competing for the choice jobs? Will he be hirable at all?

What about savings? Does Ralph have a nest egg sacked away? If so, is it big enough that he can live in the style to which he is accustomed when he leaves his current position? And what of investments? Has he made some good ones? Has he made *any*?

Does Ralph have any children still in college or graduate school? Are they still going to school on his dollar? How many more years does he have to go until they graduate?

What about children or grandchildren living at home? Or ailing parents? Or a handicapped spouse? Does Ralph have enough funds set aside to pay their medical bills? Not just bills for his dependents either—but expenses he'll have someday for himself as well.

And yes, the mortgage. Is it paid off? Or will Ralph continue to owe the bank a couple of hundred thousand for the next umpteen years?

In short, Nay wants to know: If you retire or leave your present job, how do you intend to survive?

That's Nay's inquisitional question.

Yea, meanwhile, has a different message entirely.

At your present age, Yea insists, you've got fewer life obligations than ever before.

You've put your last child through college; or you're close to it. You've paid down the mortgage; maybe even paid it off entirely. You've got tons of business network contacts, a lifetime's experience in the workplace, plus knowledge, know-how, and focus.

You've made money at your job through the years, and presumably you've invested it well enough so that you're a bit ahead of the game. You also have, or soon will have, access to cash flow from Social Security, pensions, savings, investments, real estate, and perhaps personal inherence.

The good news, therefore, is that you are in a better position to fund a new career than ever before. And you now have the financial wherewithal to manage this new line of work once it's launched.

So all things considered, says Yea, you are finally in the position you've always dreamed about. You can be your own boss at last—do your own thing; follow your own star.

Retiring? Being downsized? Losing your job?

Terrific! shouts Yea. Fantastic! These are all golden opportunities!

Think advanced home-based work technology. Think thousands of new entrepreneurial opportunities. Think franchising. Think the sheer size and power of the emerging fifty-plus work force.

Add up the advantages, Yea says, and it turns out that you are better equipped than ever before to pursue profitable self-employment. You're also better supported in this quest by society. Never in our nation's history has the climate been so friendly to post retirement entrepreneurship than it is today.

So get ready! Yea cheers you on. Your second chance is upon you. Your new life is about to begin. If you want—if you choose—if you so desire—you are now in a position to become a successful member of the Second Chance Revolution.

Forewarned is forearmed

Martha Zach, sixty-four, worked at a large hotel in Falmouth, Massachusetts, for many years. When retirement age snuck up on her, she decided to use her hotel expertise in a modest but committed way by turning several rooms of her large Victorian beach home into guest rooms and opening her own bed-and-breakfast.

After redecorating three rooms, Martha ran a rather expensive ad in *The New Yorker*, complete with a compelling photograph of her home. In it, she touted homemade meals and the great oceanfront views visitors to her bed-and-breakfast would enjoy. That was four years ago. Today, Martha's adding a wing to accommodate her waiting list of guests.

A similar success story belongs to Joseph Gooden, forty-seven. A model train enthusiast from the time he was eight, Joe dreamed of turning his hobby into a professional living. When his twenty-year stint on the Dallas Police Force came to an end, he opened a mail order model train supply store. After just fourteen months, Joe is breaking even. Next year he hopes to turn a profit.

Then there is the oft-told tale of the "ordinary American Joe," as he liked to describe himself, named Ray Kroc.

A longtime traveling salesman, Ray spent years selling Multi-Mixer milkshake machines to mom-and-pop restaurants across the United States. In his early fifties, after spending years studying the way local eating establishments delivered food to patrons, he visited a small but highly successful hamburger chain run by two brothers, Mac and Dick MacDonald. These two marketing whiz kids had developed a highly mechanized and efficient program of food preparation that they dubbed the "Speedee Service System." They were already selling franchises for their MacDonald's restaurants, though on a modest scale.

Immediately realizing the super-sized potential in the automated hamburger business, Ray went to work for the MacDonald bothers as head of franchising. After a few years, he bought them out. Once the business was his own, he surgically removed the "a" from the "Mac," changing the chain's name to McDonalds.

Ray Kroc then went on to single-handedly invent the fast food industry in America and to build the largest restaurant business in the world.

"I was fifty-two years old," Kroc wrote. "I had diabetes and incipient arthritis. I had lost my gall bladder and most of my thyroid gland in earlier campaigns, but I was convinced that the best was ahead of me."

There are countless other fifty-plus entrepreneurial success stories, some modest, some world changing, all fulfilling. You will hear many of them in the chapters to come. Yet before you start mapping out a new career, consider the less sunny side of the entrepreneurial street. Take the case of Jeffrey Starcusso.

From the day Jeffrey was hired as regional sales representative for Chrysler Motors in 1972 a small voice insistently whispered in his ear, "I'm not really cut out for office work. What I really want to do is run my own restaurant."

This voice nagged at him for three decades.

Fast forward to the year 2003.

Jeffrey's two sons are now out of college. His mortgage is paid off; he has money in the bank, investments, real estate, and a small inheritance. He has also just accepted a generous company buyout from Chrysler.

The time is ripe, he decides, to follow his entrepreneurial bliss.

Entering the restaurant trade with his usual salesman's enthusiasm, Jeffrey now proceeds to make every financial, administrative, and organizational mistake in the book.

He knows next to nothing about how the restaurant business works. Nonetheless, he fails to consult with food industry advisors or even to study up on the subject. He draws on his IRA and sells several pieces of property to fund his operation. He does this without first speaking with a financial professional.

Next, he procures the services of a commercial decorator, paying her exorbitant wages to design the high-rent space he's chosen for his business. Then, because he has spent so much of his startup nut on decor, he hires an inexperienced chef with dubious credentials to do the cooking. After the business opens, Jeffrey fails to supervise his restaurant manager properly, even when customers complain and employees keep quitting. Finally, when business-savvy friends realize that Jeffrey is on the fast lane to calamity they tender their advice. Jeffrey assures them that his problems are nothing more than growing pains, thank you very much.

Upshot?

Within two-and-a-half years Jeffrey's IRA is cashed out, his suppliers refuse to return his calls, his repeat business is minimal, his home is remortgaged, and his taxes are in a shambles. He is finally forced to close the doors of his lifetime dream for good. A few months later, he files for bankruptcy.

What caused a personal vision that seemed so right to go so wrong?

Jeffrey pursued his entrepreneurial ideal without first learning the ropes and weighing the risks.

"I took a course on entrepreneurship for six weeks at an extended learning center in Chicago," fifty-seven-year-old Sarah Martha Jacobs tells a group at a seminar on later-life employment. She is planning early retirement, she says, in search of greener pastures.

"I studied tax management for the self-employed," she explains, "financing options for startups, risk ratios for different businesses. I read about franchising, marketing, on and on. At the end of the course, my instructor asked me if I have any questions. 'Yes,' I told him. 'How do I go about approaching my ex-employer to get my old job back?'"

Moral: When contemplating later-life entrepreneurship, don't leap before you look.

But also, be of good cheer. One out of six working men and women over the age of fifty is currently self-employed, and twelve percent of workers over sixty own their own business. From our perspective at the Lawrence N. Field Center for Entrepreneurship, many fifty-plus entrepreneurs appear to be enjoying themselves immensely and are also profiting financially from their new ventures. Their success is due to knowledge and hard work, definitely. But just as importantly, it results from a thorough understanding of the risks and rewards exclusive to entrepreneurship at their particular stage in life.

Whatever work options you may currently entertain, the first prerequisite is to understand the pros and cons of self-employment from the vantage point of who—and where—you are today. Here's some advice that will help.

Five critical things to think about before starting your own business at fifty and over

Popular wisdom tells us that most small businesses fail.

This belief, like many others in the rogues' gallery of popular wisdom, is incorrect.

According to figures provided by Dun and Bradstreet, approximately one percent of small businesses in the United States are forced to close every year. Doing the math, this means that ninety-nine percent remain open. At worst, these small businesses are barely squeezing by. At best, they are booming.

No statistical findings that we know of reveal the precise percent of entrepreneurial success stories that can be attributed to persons over fifty. Nevertheless, indications are that older entrepreneurs make better entrepreneurs, for reasons that will be discussed below.

Still, there are issues to think about seriously before taking the plunge. Five of the most important are listed below. This list is not designed to be discouraging. Mr. Nay is by no means running the show. It is presented simply as food for thought, along with the other information and advice presented in this book, to help you gain as broad and comprehensive a picture of entrepreneurship as possible before making any major decisions.

Consider for example:

1. Are you ready to make the transition from mother ship to sailboat?

If you've been working in a company or corporate environment for many years, you have become accustomed to certain amenities. You may even take them for granted.

For example, when your computer crashes, a tech person is always there to fix it. When you go home at night, someone vacuums the floor around your desk. Come the end of the week, you have a paycheck waiting for you. Come the end of the year, you have a paid vacation and perhaps a bonus. You have health and insurance benefits and perhaps other perks such as a company car or membership in a health club.

These are attractive sweeteners to anyone's work-a-day routine, and habits die hard. When such perks are no longer available, which they decidedly are not for persons running their own commercial operations, they are missed.

A series of questions we therefore ask retirement-age people who have comfortably ridden a corporate mother ship for many years include the following:

- Are you a "self-starter"? Do you have the initiative to move projects forward without pressure from a boss or co-workers?
- Are you ready to do it yourself? Are you prepared to use QuickBooks, pay quarterly payroll taxes, equip an office, and set up databases? If not, have you budgeted enough in your business plan to pay someone to do these things for you?
- Are you comfortable working by yourself all day long? Are you willing, if necessary, to put in long hours alone at night?
- Do you have enough knowledge of office machines to fix them when they go down? If not, is there room in your budget for paying a tech person?
- Are you temperamentally fit to deal with the stress that comes from being your own boss, carrying the weight of an entire business on your shoulders, waiting for critical answers, and managing complex cash flow?
- Are you willing to do whatever it takes to make your business succeed, including making deliveries on your own, cleaning your office, and taking packages to the post office?
- Are your energy level steady and your state of health good? Do you feel up to the physical task of running your own business?
- If your business fails or falters, are you able to lose lots of money and still be the same cheerful, happy person your family and friends now know and love?

There are no right or wrong answers to these questions. But there are indicative yes and no answers. If you have a high proportion of nos, further self-questioning may be in order before making any commitments.

2. Do you fit the entrepreneurial prototype?

Technically speaking, there is no such thing as an entrepreneurial prototype. Different businesses require different (and sometimes opposing) temperaments. For example, a dealer who sells antiques on a home computer needs a different set of secretarial and social skills than a person who sells the same items at flea markets every weekend.

Such differences notwithstanding, there are still a number of general skills that are valuable for *all* types of entrepreneurial enterprises. A representative list includes:

- Flexibility and the capacity to adapt to change.
- A reasonable education, especially a business-related education. This is by no means a prerequisite; however, for large-scale independent business ventures it helps. Among people in the fifty-plus category, education can also simply mean having a good deal of prior business experience.
- Optimism and a can-do attitude. Also optimism's inverse: resilience—the ability to absorb disappointments, setbacks, and reversals without becoming discouraged. "Bounce-backability" is the way one sixty-eight-year-old entrepreneur described it to me.
- Good interpersonal skills, with an outgoing personality highlighted by a friendly, no-ax-to-grind attitude.
- Organizational skills. An ability to see the big picture and a complementary capacity for paying attention to details.
- Basic managerial competence—especially the ability to manage cash flow, set up business systems, and keep a commercial operation running at an efficient day-to-day pace.
- Intuition, inventiveness, the ability to use time well, and a decent sized portion of self-confidence.

Nobody is going to have all the above skills, of course, and indeed, not all the above skills are necessary for every business. Most fifty-plus entrepreneurs will possess some of these skills though. If you feel you have none of them, this can be a red flag. If you think you have a few, well, many of the others can be learned as you go along.

What is most important when measuring your own business potential is self-knowledge—assessing your skills, personality, and current life situation with an objective eye, then determining how well suited your best interests are to the demands of self-employment. The information in Chapter 2 will help guide you.

3. Are you prepared to transition from a group way of thinking to an individual way of thinking?

Psychologists Robert Kagan and Lisa L. Lahey, in their article "Adult Leadership and Adult Development,"[1] suggest that people accustomed to company rules and policy are given the opportunity at retirement age to make a crossover into what they term the "post institutional identity."

From our earliest days, Kagan and Lahey argue, we are socialized to think group and to group-think. High school, college, office, community, and all the other hieratical institutions that organize our lives insist that we view ourselves as a single dot in a web of dots, all interconnected by the lines of rules, relationships, and social agreements.

Once retirement age approaches, Kagan and Lahey say, we can step out of this web or at least step back from it. In the process, we automatically become more independent and self-starting. When retirement time arrives, the authors suggest, it may be time to start thinking "I" more and "we" less. Once this step is taken, once we view ourselves less as a part and more as a whole, self-employment starts to make real sense.

4. How much risk is too much risk?

Because it is more difficult to replenish capital and to rebuild a monetary base at age sixty-one than at age twenty-four, people at retirement age are often less willing to put their finances on the line and major downturns like those of 2008–2009 make everyone more fragile financially. True, those over age fifty are probably less hasty and less likely to make foolish financial decisions than their younger counterparts, but they are also more financially vulnerable.

How then, do you find the balance point? What are the safest ways to bankroll a startup business at this point in life? How much money can you afford to lose and still stay comfortably solvent?

---

[1] Doctorial dissertation presented at Antioch College, Ohio Department of Philosophy. To read this article see *www.ohiolink.edu/etd/self-pdf.cgi?antioch*1165860089.

In Chapter 2 we take you though a step-by-step money management analysis to help determine the degree of risk you can safely assume to get your business launched. If after reading this section you feel that even a little business risk is too much business risk, it may be better to use your hard-earned money in safer and more protected ways.

5. Is there an entrepreneurial career specifically geared to your current life needs?

Many aspiring fifty-plus entrepreneurs know what type of business they want to start. Others simply know that they want to start a business.

For people in the second group, Chapter 2 reviews the types of entrepreneurial businesses that are most popular with people over fifty. It explains how these businesses work, the personal and business skills that are needed for each, and the compensations one can expect to reap at the tunnel's end. These categories include franchises, retail operations, trades, consulting, home-based businesses, service-oriented businesses, and several others.

Go over the entries in this chapter carefully. If and when the shoe fits, consider putting it on. If none of these generic business categories excites you, keep looking.

At the same time, the very fact that none of the offerings listed in this chapter appeals to you may be a tip-off. Most members of the Second Chance Revolution are actively seeking careers that satisfy both their commercial ambitions and their emotional dispositions. It's Freud's "work and love" thesis once more. If none of the businesses profiled in Chapter 2 fulfills either of these needs—and if after more searching you still don't discover a business you feel you'd be happy spending the next several years pursuing—perhaps entrepreneurship is not in the cards for you at the present time.

Nine good reasons why fifty-plus entrepreneurship is in the cards for you

So much for the cautions.

Here is a list of compelling reasons why the time has never been riper for you to go independent, and why entrepreneurship is so attractive to so many people in the middle and later years. Note that some of the considerations listed below have been mentioned in one context or another already. We are mentioning them again because they are important. Read and consider.

1. You're smarter now and better connected than you've ever been in all your life.

"With aging comes sage-ing," as the saying goes.

Which means that during your years at the office—or at the store, or at the site, or in the field, or behind the counter, or on the phone, or on the road—you have acquired abilities, wisdom, and contacts you may not even know you possess. You already have a ready reference encyclopedia of professional knowledge inside your head. You have acquired a sharpened sense of business (and personal) psychology, as well as a set of expectations made reasonable in the fiery forge of worldly experience. Through the years, you may have also distilled a sense of humor—and probably tolerance as well—about your own shortcomings and about those of the people you work with. You know the score.

Blend these skills and insights together and you get, if you'll pardon the boring phrase, a "mature attitude"—the kind that takes half a lifetime to acquire. "Only in our maturity," the German poet Goethe once remarked, "can we understand what happened to us in our youth." This attitude automatically makes you better at what you do, especially when it comes to business, finance, and social interaction. It just works that way.

2. Entrepreneurship is now open to everyone.

Two decades ago, the word "entrepreneur" made you think of Daddy Warbucks type investors doling out millions from penthouse offices. During the Internet boom of the 1990s, entrepreneurship spoke of quick ramp-ups, complex business plans for untested technology, courting overly optimistic capitalists, making a quick kill, and cashing out pronto.

Today the concept of entrepreneurship has changed. It still conjures images of high finance. It also makes us think of home offices, family businesses, small investment startups, local franchises, building a better mousetrap in the garage, and seeking after modest but satisfying lifestyle goals.

A white paper prepared by the Small Business Administration several years ago[2] found that sixty-nine percent of new jobs in the United States are created by startup businesses. Business schools that focused exclusively on preparing students for work at major corporations now emphasize entrepreneurial training. Such changes in commerce and education make later-life entrepreneurship more accessible and acceptable than ever before, especially for retirement-age people who do not want to retire.

3. Technology makes it easier than ever before to run a business from home.

For years, the first thing you had to do when starting a new business was to rent office space (let's see now, 1,200 square feet at *how many* dollars per foot?), then hire a staff, purchase office furniture, take out insurance, decorate, and lay in vast stocks of paperclips and paper towels.

Why the effort and expense?

Because having a formal walk-in office was considered the only way to make your new enterprise "real."

Meanwhile, what about working at home?

This option was scowled at by the professional world. "Home offices," I recall a rich investor once telling me, "are for people who're afraid of dealing directly with the world."

Today, of course, computers, printers, fax machines, automatic telephone answering, email, and the Internet have changed all that, making home-based businesses manageable, inexpensive, and if you so desire, part-time as well. They offer an ideal second-career headquarters for workplace veterans who are tired of commuting or of the maze of gray cubicles. For a number of fifty-plussers, their "office" now consists of a computer—period. Indeed, sometimes all they need is a phone.

---

[2] See the Small Business Administration's website at *www.sba.gov/starting_business/startup/guide.html*.

4. You're now in an excellent financial position to work for yourself.

If you have been vigilant with your finances, you have probably saved some money. You may also be heir to capital from pensions due, retirement plans, stock sharing, inheritance, Social Security, and other age-related payoffs.

Chances are, therefore, that you are in a reasonably sound financial position to take judicious financial risks. Chapter 3 delves in greater detail into the question of risk, personal finances, and ways to fund business startups.

5. Knowledge-based businesses are now in high demand.

Outsourcing was once considered a bad word. Today it is recognized as an efficient way to do business. This sea of change is a boon for later-life entrepreneurs who can now use their skills, knowledge, and education to become independent contractors or to set up their own consulting operations.

In the Information Age, knowledge is as saleable a commodity as cars and houses. People over fifty have a particularly large stockpile of goods.

6. Entrepreneurship trumps ageism.

Attitudes toward older people in the work force, shadowed for so many years by the clichés of ageism, are becoming increasingly positive. Perhaps it is simply that there is power in numbers, and that the sheer volume of people over fifty who are opting to remain wage earners is creating new norms. Whatever the case, the climate in the business community is turning friendly toward older workers. So is the support and encouragement of society.

At the same time, if you decide to work past retirement age, there is always a chance that ageism will rear its grouchy head, especially if you seek employment at a company or corporation. Here's another reason why entrepreneurship is such an attractive option: It frees you from age-related bias and allows you to set your own agenda. When you become your own boss, the only one who decides how long you will keep working is you.

7. Capital investment sources have become increasingly friendly to fifty-plus businesses.

Bill Payne, a consultant at the Kauffman Foundation and an investor in startup businesses for twenty years, reports seeing a marked increase in boomer-led companies searching for seed money. He himself prefers funding such companies, he tells us, because the people behind these startups usually come to him with such a large war chest of expertise and experience.

"Speaking as an investor who looks at hundreds of business plans per quarter," said Payne, "we are encouraged when we see some senior guys who have a lot of vertical experience. We know they're bringing business savvy and that they're reasonable, rational people. We definitely are seeing more people in the boomer age bracket."

Banks, lending institutions, private organizations, and angel investors increasingly share Bill Payne's enthusiasms. "A lot of the smart investment money," a private lender recently told me, "is going to the business veterans these days. They know what to do with the money better than the younger set."

8. You can make your new business a family affair and pass down the values and rewards.

For many years, you've worked to support your family. Now you can work *with* your family—with a spouse, partner, children, brothers, sisters, cousins, and aunts.

This ready-made staff automatically becomes the beneficiary of your business expertise and monetary investment. In turn, you have employees whom you like and trust. Keeping it all in the family gives you the opportunity to teach loved ones what you have learned in business through the years and to pass on your legacy of knowledge to future generations.

Finally, later on, when you retire, or when you leave on a more permanent basis, the business you've built with your relatives can become a source of family income and fulfillment for years to come.

When set up and administered properly, a family business is a win-win deal. In Chapter 8 we show you how to do it.

9. You can set your own level of time and involvement.
A major benefit of fifty-plus entrepreneurship is that you can tailor-make a business to fit your personal schedule.

You can, for example, decide how many hours per week you'll work and then spend the rest of the time with family and friends. You can choose to do business with partners, or you can go it alone. You can focus on current income or on building future value. You can work at home or at an outside office.

Few people in all history have been privy to such a wide range of occupational options as they are today. Take advantage of them.

The answers to your questions

Becoming your own boss when over fifty is unlike any business venture you have undertaken before. It comes with its own particular set of satisfactions, demands, and rewards, all of which are different from those experienced in earlier life. And so, the big questions again:

1. Should I do it?

Hopefully, after reading this chapter you've decided that entrepreneurship is your ship to sail. Or, better said perhaps, your plane to fly. From now on, we are going to make the assumption that you wish to become an entrepreneur. To paraphrase the message at take-off: This plane is flying to entrepreneurship today. If your destination is not entrepreneurship, we suggest that you leave the plane immediately.

2. Which business should I choose?

Your choice of business depends on many things, including your skills and talents, your past work experience, your current financial situation, your available time, your family practicalities, your tax position, your network of contacts, your estate-planning wishes, your personal health and energy quota, your individual goals, your ambition level, your place of residence, and more. In the next chapter, we will help you narrow down these choices so you can target the career that's best suited to your specific temperament, needs, and abilities.

3. What important things will I know after reading this book?

After you read this book, your new-and-improved knowledge base will include information from a fifty-plus perspective on a number of important issues. These include choosing an appropriate entrepreneurial career; financing a startup business; negotiating tax, insurance, and legal issues; setting up a home office; developing marketing strategies; writing a business plan; investing in a franchise; learning to share and network with others; the ins and outs of operating a family business; and the best ways of building value in a business for your heirs.

Most importantly, after reading the chapters that follow you will enter the world of entrepreneurship from a position of knowledge rather than guesswork, assumption, and magical thinking. You will be prepared.

4. Where do I go from here?

That's the best part.

In the chapters to come, we'll tell you all about it.

Chapter 2
Choosing an Entrepreneurial Profession That's Right for You

Making the key decisions
You've weighed the options, you've pondered the pros and cons, and you've decided to go entrepreneurial.

Very good. Entrepreneurship is good, especially at that certain moment at midlife or beyond when so many of us are so very ready for a change. During the course of the years, we've seen hundreds of men and women over fifty who've become their own bosses, and who have benefited from this decision in a number of financial and personal ways. Entrepreneurship has the potential to change your life for the better.

Once resolved to start your own business, what's more, this decision opens the door to several more choices, all of them critical. The fact is, the way you negotiate key issues during the early stages of a business startup will be a major factor in determining whether your venture will get off the ground—or go into it.

Get it right from the start
Some years ago in a PBS interview, the famous scholar and mythologist, Joseph Campbell, was asked what advice he would offer people seeking direction in life. "Follow your bliss," Campbell replied. "When you follow your bliss," he added, "you put yourself on a kind of track

which has been there all the while waiting for you, and the life that you ought to be living is the one you are now living."

Good advice.

No, *great* advice. Do the thing you love most. Go for the gold.

Teresa M. Amabile, professor of business administration at Harvard University, agrees. Professor Amabile has studied human creativity for a number of years. One of her major conclusions is that people soar to their highest creative peaks when working at a job they love.

Based on this premise, Professor Amabile makes a distinction between what she calls "intrinsic" and "extrinsic" motivation.

Intrinsic motivation takes place when people develop a fire in their belly for a particular occupation, a fire that originates entirely from within. Extrinsic motivation comes into play when outside forces mold a person's professional incentives; forces such as praise, financial reward, and health benefits. Controlled psychological studies, Professor Amabile tells us, show that intrinsic motivation is a far more effective tool than extrinsic for stimulating professional excellence.

Thus, if you derive intense enjoyment from a recreational pastime like my friend Frank, the ex-banker turned stamp merchant, it's natural to want to involve yourself in this activity on a permanent basis. People like Frank have always known that, given their druthers, they would turn their bliss-making diversion into a career. When the Franks of the world reach a point in life when it finally becomes possible to do this, their choice of careers comes ready-made. They will morph their hobby into dollars. End of story.

At the same time, there's a great deal more to career change than following your bliss. Let's make it clear from the start: Joseph Campbell's advice is relevant only when you know what your bliss actually is.

For those at the over-fifty crossroads who are not so sure, and who are motivated less by turning a passion into a profession and more by simply finding a rewarding second career, choosing requires serious self-analysis and self-questioning. This process begins and ends in the competitive marketplace where the approximately fifteen–twenty percent of retirement-age Americans who wish to start their own business are regaled with a selection of career choices that appears, for all intents and purposes, limitless.

Books with titles hawking *300 of the Fastest Growing Professions in the United States, 500 Great Businesses You Can Run at Home, 1,000 Fabulous Entrepreneurial Startups,* and so forth beckon from the shelves of every Borders and Barnes & Noble bookstore. There are, in fact, so many opportunities that at times it seems the biggest job of all is to simply sift through this mountain of career choices until you find a few realistic possibilities. While this task may seem a tall order, discovering an ideal second career is really quite doable, especially if the search is focused on personal fulfillment as well as monetary need.

To move you along in this area, a career selection guide is presented below.

This series of questions and suggestions is designed to help you eliminate the career choices that do *not* meet your standards and to identify the ones that *do.* Give each of the items in this guide the attention it deserves and by the sheer process of elimination you'll soon have an attractive shortlist of possible careers.

Career selection guide for the fifty-plus entrepreneur

1. Master the basics.

Begin with the personal and financial fundamentals that underlie any career decision. For example:

- **Find a business you really like.** It sounds incredible, but studies tell us that at as many as forty percent of later-life entrepreneurs invest their time and money in a business they take no pride in owning and no pleasure in operating. You don't have to adore the business you choose. But you darn well better like it.
- **Ask yourself: What type of work do I enjoy most and what type of work do I do best?** What would I do if I could wave a magic wand and have any career in the world? What are my special interests, talents, hankerings, and areas of learning? What are my best traits—friendliness, persuasiveness, patience, will power, creativity? How might they be put to work in a specific profession? Which of my professional skills give me the most potential star power?

What interesting business ideas have I considered in the past that I might like to pursue today?

- **Free associate.** See yourself working at a job you deeply enjoy. Snap a mental picture of yourself doing your dream—designing dresses, choreographing numbers in a dance studio, holding a camera in a photography emporium, setting type on a hand-operated printing press, lecturing before a crowd, wiring a house, selling insurance, retailing antiques, operating a farm, taking care of children, delivering health care services, writing magazine articles, running a restaurant, coaching a team, helping the homeless—whatever turns you on.

    Now write down the most appealing and realistic of these images. Consider ways in which you might turn one or more of them into a career.

    Then take a walk, go for a run, work out at the gym, listen to music, do a crossword, take a cat nap, read a magazine article, make a drawing, soak in a bathtub, or take a dip in a pool. Let the ideas and images percolate through your brain for a while.

    Then think about it all again.

    Gradually, new ideas will come on their own, sometimes at the most surprising times and in the most surprising places. Let the creative process do the work for you. Your job is to program the creative parts of your mind with the raw materials of career change. Then sit back and see what ideas pop up.

- **Solicit opinions from people you respect.** Write a formal one-page description of the business choices that appeal to you most. Pass on this page to friends, business associates, family members, and potential customers—anyone who can give you helpful, honest advice.

    Ask for their comments. What choices do they think are best suited to your personality and lifestyle? What choices do they think are all wrong for you? What other types of business might they suggest? What related ideas can they give you? What jobs do they think you're best suited for? What mistakes do they think you might be making?

Once you get the feedback, take the good advice to heart and forget about the rest. Then keep looking and thinking and be patient. You've probably been moving in the direction of a new career for many years without consciously knowing it. It takes time to hit the bull's eye.

2. **Try the SCAMPER technique.** SCAMPER is an acronym that stands for:
Substitute
Combine
Adapt
Modify
Put
Eliminate
Reverse

A creative thinking exercise designed by educator, Bob Eberle, SCAMPER is designed to help people solve a wide range of problems. It can be used, its fans tell us, to plot a story, design a computer, play a better game of chess, or win a war. It can definitely be used by people who are searching for a new vocation, and/or who wish to fine-tune their new business once they discover it.

The items in the SCAMPER acronym work like this:

Substitute: Devise a better idea for a business by replacing—and/or improving on—the systems and materials currently used by the competition. For instance, if you want to manufacture a new and innovative stereo speaker, consider substituting wood casings for plastic. If you're thinking of opening a movie theater, how about installing a computerized ticket-taking apparatus to free up employees for more important jobs.

Combine: Can you take the best parts of other businesses and unite them into a bigger, better business? If you intend to open a food shop, why not include a sushi counter, a catering service, and/or a wine-tasting (and selling) kiosk to attract more customers. If you plan to start a manicure and pedicure salon, consider offering foot massages and back rubs as value-added services to attract customers.

Adapt: You improve on a business by making it attractive to a wider market and/or to a larger customer base. You might, for example, turn a seasonal ice skating rink into a year-round enclosed rink. You might open a gourmet food market with foods on the shelf that appeal to persons from other cultures as well as to Americans.

Modify: Change (and thus improve) an essential feature of a product such as its size, ingredients, color, packaging, or price. Try, for instance, selling brownies with nuts rather than plain. Open a gift basket business that includes flowers, plants, and hard-to-find food items in its selection.

Put (to other uses): Can you alter your business or product in such a way that it provides more than one good or service? Besides offering custom sound systems, you might also sell a technical service like product testing. If you start a miniature golf course, think of renting the course out after hours for private parties or business events.

Eliminate: Prune the dead wood. If three persons get the job done crafting your new line of jewelry and you're employing five, cut the roster. If plants sell better in a nursery than fresh-cut flowers, deep six the flowers and concentrate on items your customers want most.

Reverse: Reverse conventional wisdom. For example, buy speakers from other manufacturers, and then only provide marketing and distribution. If you open a liquor store, install a bar in the back to serve drinks.

> A good website for learning creative thinking about topics such as career change is *www.mycoted.com/creativity/techniques/index.php*. The section on idea generation is especially helpful. You'll see SCAMPER mentioned here as one of the techniques.

3. Study other successful businesses.

Wherever you go, take note. Why is the shop on 4th Street always brimful of customers? Why is the shop on 5th Street always empty? What are these businesses doing that boosts—or retards—their sales?

4. Strategize how you would do things better than the competition.

- **Ask yourself:** What underserved markets can I tap into? Consider especially growing and expanding underserved markets.

- **Think:** What local products and services frustrate me most when I use them? Does the local dry cleaner do a careless job of cleaning my sweaters? Does the town wine merchant offer a puny selection of white wines? Does the hardware store on Main Street cater too much to tradesmen and not enough to homeowners? Does the town pizza taste like an old shoe? What local goods and service businesses—or more ambitiously, what state or national businesses—need improvement?
- **Do the necessary research.** Attend trade shows, visit showrooms, talk to people involved in the careers in which you're interested. Read business-oriented newspapers like *Barron's* and *The Wall Street Journal*. Check out government records such as patent information and agency reports. Peruse trade magazines, brochures, reports, and advertising materials in the fields of business that interest you. Let everything you see and read and learn percolate through your mental filtering system. Sometimes simply being in the vicinity of opportunity creates opportunity. As comedian/director Woody Allen once remarked, "Ninety percent of success is just showing up."

Nutshell advice for beginning entrepreneurs

There's no such thing as the perfect marriage, the perfect wave, *or* the perfect business. Every entrepreneurial venture comes with a downside and an up. Your task is to find a new profession with more ups than downs. Here's a back-of-the matchbook recipe for some things to consider:

1. Find a business you like doing—a lot.
2. Find a business that takes full advantage of the talents and knowledge you already have.
3. Find a business that best suits your time schedule.
4. Find a business that can earn you enough money.
5. Find a business that allows you to work in a location and environment you most prefer.

- **Ask yourself: Do you possess an unusual skill that gives you an advantage in certain business ventures?** Perhaps, for example, you speak Chinese. In today's international marketplace, skill at Cantonese or Mandarin can open certain doors. So can fluency in German, Arabic, Japanese, and a dozen other languages widely used in the business world. Or, let's say you're a part-time magician who performs magic shows at children's birthday parties. Did you, like many children interested in magic, learn to juggle when you were young? If so, don't let this skill go unused. Juggling can be that extra asset that makes your kiddie show stand out from the competition.

5. Decide how many hours a week you want to work.

While some members of the fifty-plus generation approach a new profession full steam ahead, others prefer to slacken the pace and to, well, just plain not work so long and hard.

If you want to reduce your workload, search for a business that gives you control over both your clients and your schedule. Choose a business that permits you to take the day off when the spirit (or a grandchild) moves you. Choose a business that allows you to leave work early or to go on last-minute vacations. Distance yourself from the tyranny of the punch clock.

America offers its workforce fewer vacation days than any other country in the Western world (in most European countries companies are legally obliged to give employees six weeks vacation a year). To add to this privation, American workers also give back approximately *20 billion dollars* each year to their employers. How? By not using the vacation time that's due them. Primary reason cited: "I'm too busy."

Remember, vacation time is that slim, precious slice of the year when you recharge and revive. Vacations prevent burnout and compound well-being. They keep you healthy—that's important. It's estimated that 72 million Americans suffer from work-related health problems every year, such as ulcers, anxiety, stroke, and heart attacks. How many of these ailments might be avoided by taking a few weeks rest. Make sure you choose a business that obliges your needs in this department.

There are many entrepreneurial professions that allow people to self-manage their time schedules. Most are home-based. A sampling includes:

Astrologer	Desktop publisher	Grant writer
Consultant	Translator	Photographer
Appliance repair	Beekeeper	Clown
Newsletter writer	Rubber stamp business	Tax accountant (seasonal)
Seamstress	Website designer	Lawn care service (seasonal)
Upholsterer	Mail order company	Computer repair service
Home crafts	Furniture maker	Home manicure service
Tutor	Writer	Illustrator

In general, young entrepreneurs rarely concern themselves with cutting back on their time. They know they want to succeed, and they know they want to make money. They'll work 60 hours a week to do it. Fifty-plus entrepreneurs, on the other hand, are often willing to earn less in order to work less. They've put in their time over the years. Now they want some extra hours in the day for themselves. Such people benefit by setting specific time goals and by mapping a schedule strategy. A typical fifty-plus time-management scenario might read like this:

- I want to work thirty hours a week. (I don't want to work any longer than this.)
- I want to earn $15,000–$20,000 a year. (I don't need to work any harder than this.)
- I want two months off during the summer (non-negotiable).
- I want to take a week off at Christmas (and maybe spring break as well).
- I want several weeks of vacation in the winter (or fall or spring).
- I want to give myself the option of cutting back on work hours at any time of the year. (Eat your hearts out, nine-to-fivers!)

Here are a few helpful thoughts on effective time management:
- Chose a business in which you can hire a manager as the main service deliverer. This strategy gets you off the work hook to the extent that you want to get off—and to the extent that your manager is competent and willing to work.
- Take a seasonal job, such as driveway snow removal or running a nursery. Keep the remaining months of the year for yourself.
- Purchase a franchise and let your manager and employees assume the burden of work. (This is a tricky one. We will discuss franchises at length in Chapter 7.)
- Start a family business. From the beginning, make it clear to all family employees that you intend to work X number of hours a week. (The ins and outs of family businesses are discussed in Chapter 8.)

6. Ask yourself: What type of business arrangement do I prefer: a startup, a buyout, or a franchise?

We will talk a good deal about the feasibility of each of these business models in upcoming chapters. For the time being, simply keep this question on your radar screen.

7. Where you sit is where you fit.

The place where you spend eight hours a day, or ten hours, or two is critical to job satisfaction. Ask yourself: If given the choice, what type of work environment do I most prefer?

Some independent businesses require that you to spend your entire workday in an office. Others allow you to run a business in your garage, basement, bedroom, or attic. Some let you work part-time at home and in an office the rest of the time. Some take you to a warehouse or factory. Other businesses, such as a messenger service or a golf instructor service, bring you outdoors. Some demand that you drive a vehicle for long distances. Others entail traveling abroad.

Which type of work location is most in tune with your vision of the ideal job? Which the least?

8. Ask yourself: Do I prefer working by myself or with other people?

Do you enjoy interacting with others during the day? Do you prefer working with a partner? With family members? A staff? How large or small a staff?

Certain entrepreneurial professions demand that you be a "people person"; that you know how to sell yourself, to make a splash; that you enjoy hanging out with business associates at the end of the day. Others limit your public interface to electronic communications only—to the telephone, fax, email, and Internet. Are you a people person? A loner? A bit of both? Which set of work conditions best suits your personality?

Weigh and consider these questions—they're important—and add your conclusions to the mix.

9. Ask yourself: How much money can I afford to spend on a new business?

Think about your basic needs: office files, computers, printers, advertising, furniture, water coolers, business stationery, payroll, benefits, and erasers, whatever. Make a preliminary list, then do a ballpark estimate of how much it will all cost. At this point, these figures are not final. They're just a seat-of-the pants way of figuring out what you can and cannot afford.

10. Ask yourself: How much financial risk am I willing to take?

Entrepreneurial risk means, well, risk. To put it in question form: What are the chances that your new business will succeed or fail?

Basically, there are three levels of safety in any entrepreneurial adventure: low, medium, and high. Decide which of these levels you are most comfortable assuming, and look for a business that fits.

Typical examples of low-, medium-, and high-risk professions include:

Low Risk
- Independent consultant

- Small home-based business (such as accounting, arts/crafts, tutoring, tarot card reading, monogramming service, lead solder foundry, marriage counseling, home beauty salon)
- Online business (like eBay or your own commercial website)

Medium Risk
- Provider of local community services such as a taxi delivery service
- Investment in an existing small business
- Product-based business such as selling Mary Kay cosmetics
- Independent contracting services in the trades—plumbing, landscaping, electrical

High Risk
- Storefront retail business (including restaurants)
- Franchises
- Inventing (and sometimes marketing) new products

The level of risk you are willing to take depends on your economic situation at this stage of your life. If you have ample savings and a large war chest, a high-risk business may be your game—but not always. With careful choices, a little can be a lot.

Conversely, you may have more money to invest than you think; or you may be better positioned to move into a medium- or even high-risk business than you suppose.

11. Ask yourself: Where will I find my funding sources?

Where is the money for your new project coming from? From the bank, from loan institutions, from backers, friends, relatives? From your own savings and investments? Given the financial turmoil of recent times, are your savings still intact? Do you have enough in the bank to cover the bases?

The money question is always the 800-pound gorilla, especially in the middle or later years if, heaven forbid, one's new entrepreneurial venture should tank. If this happens, entrepreneurs stand to lose part or all of their hard-earned savings. Needless to say, starting again financially is not so easy. The art and science of finding funding is discussed in detail in Chapter 3.

12. Keep looking, keep talking to people, and don't get discouraged.

After studying the market and scoping out what it is that Americans really wanted and needed, two young engineers at Hewlett-Packard had a bright idea: make a desk-sized, user-friendly computer that can be used at home and in the office. They took this far-out notion to their bosses—who promptly shot it down. Undaunted, Steve Jobs and Steve Wozniak founded their own company. They called it Apple Computer.

Arthur Blank was fired from the building supply company where he had worked for many years. Getting downsized gave him an idea—start an all-under-one-roof building-supply company that caters to homeowners as well as builders. He looked around, talked to people, and did his research. No such store existed. His would be the first. Result: Home Depot.

A Texas saleswoman worked diligently in the cosmetics industry for many years. She talked to customers each day about their cosmetic preferences and passed this valuable information on to her bosses. But when promotion time came around she found herself hitting the glass ceiling. She was never going to be promoted to sales manager, she realized, because she was a woman. So Mary Kay started her own business: Mary Kay Cosmetics.

By the time he turned sixty Andrew J. McKelvey had already started a string of businesses. Some of them were successful, some were not. One day, after scouring the Internet for career opportunities, he concluded that the job-finding potential of the Internet was not being fully exploited. He then came up with the idea of a broad-based online career agency and named it Monster.com. The rest is history. "What you do in business is follow your nose," McKelvey once said by way of offering advice to aspiring entrepreneurs. "The secret of success is being at the right place at the right time with the right idea." You get the idea. Keep looking, keep thinking, and keep bouncing your ideas off other people. Don't get discouraged.

Look for a new business that uses the work skills and experience you've already acquired

You've spent your entire professional life as a mortgage broker, let us say. You're approaching retirement age. You decide that now you'd like to open a flower shop or start a microbrewery.

There's nothing wrong with these new career paths. However, unless you've been raising and selling flowers in your backyard for years, or unless you've taken courses on brewing science and possess the administrative savvy to run a small factory, these choices, so far afield of your established knowledge and information base, can sink your ship before it's launched.

Here's a better idea: Use the work-related skills and experience you already possess.

Free help getting started

Would-be entrepreneurs in their fifties, sixties, and seventies sometimes feel intimidated by the many new business skills they must master. Drawing up business plans, raising money, keeping records, managing one's time and one's staff can be daunting challenges, especially at the beginning. Happily, there are organizations that offer free counsel and advice. Check at your local schools, community centers, job fairs, and colleges. Try Googling sources in your area, and checking out magazines like *Entrepreneur, Inc.* Go online to *www.vFinance.com*.

Organizations that offer free entrepreneurial advice, information, and sometimes one-on-one counseling for fifty-plus entrepreneurs include the following:

- AARP *www.aarp.org*
- The Kauffman Foundation (*www.fasttrac.org*) (offers the FastTrac business-development program for aspiring entrepreneurs)
- Service Corps of Retired Executives (SCORE) (*www.score.org*) (SCORE has more than 10,500 volunteer counselors across the country to guide beginning entrepreneurs)
- International Franchise Association (*www.franchise.org*)
- KCSourceLink (866-870-6500) or (*www.kcsourcelink.com*) (especially for people from Missouri and the Midwest)
- Mid-America Minority Business Development Council (*www.mambdc.org*)

- Small Business Administration (*www.sba.gov*) (provides many services and, in some cases, funding for entrepreneurs)

For example, if you have worked as a mortgage broker for many years and you feel it's time to move on, choose a career that's related to your existing knowledge base. Seek opportunity in land development or as a real estate agent. You might also enjoy working as an editor at a magazine devoted to real estate, as an independent mortgage consultant, or even as a financial advisor. Unless you are already well versed in these professions, it does *not* make sense, for instance, to open a grocery store or a dog kennel.

Recently *www.satisfactionmag.com*, an e-zine dedicated to lifestyle issues for people over fifty, featured an interview with Jim Chambliss, a diagnostic radiologist who opted to start a new career after thirty-five years working at the same job. His choice? Medical informatics, a profession that acquires, stores, and retrieves health care information.

"You know when it's time to end your primary career," Chambliss tells us. "You get lots of signals. Some are internal and some are external. When it gets to that point, you don't want to spend your life doing nothing. You feel like you are still useful, so you look around and think, 'What can I do?' Sometimes it's something that pops up, like this medical informatics deal, which is not a far cry from what I was doing. Last year, I saw that Northwestern was establishing a master's degree program in medical informatics for people with my background. I said, 'Why not?'"

The key point is that Chambliss, like other canny fifty-plus entrepreneurs, knows he can make a seamless career transition by building on his pre-existing foundation of expertise and experience.

"You look for things where you have a foundation," Chambliss tells us. "So it's not quite as difficult as [when you have] no background. Medical information is not entirely new to me."

Make a list. Jot down your special business talents and your strongest areas of experience. Also, make note of the areas of trade and commerce you are most qualified to practice. List what you already know about running certain businesses, and make note of the people you know in these fields. This exercise should help give you a clear

idea of the type of professions you're most suited to pursue. If "follow your bliss" is the mantra for youthful newbie entrepreneurs, "follow your bliss *along with* your expertise" should be the theme for every aspiring businessperson over fifty.

A kissing cousin of the section above, finding a second career over fifty is automatically made easier for you because you already know so many people in your field. Do not—repeat, do not—neglect this important support when choosing a new career.

Check your address book. Read it through as if you were perusing a gripping novel. Make note of the people and/or organizations that you know, that you have worked with in the past, and that may be in a position to help today. Think business network. Think social network. Focus on sources from your pool of family, friends, work associates, and past co-workers. A well-stocked Rolodex is sometimes all you need to get started in the right business.

◂ The circa-1930s ad to the left is an amusing example of how product appeal can change dramatically through the years. Tobacco smoking as a gentile, manly pastime, pipes as aphrodisiacs, ambient smoke fumes as perfume, and certain assumptions about female romantic tastes (along with the mandatory college study of Greek) are all things of the past. To make the right entrepreneurial decisions always look to the present—and to the future.

When searching for a business with high success potential, look for one that fills a present and urgent need

During the last years of the Roman Republic, Marcus Licinius Crassus, a businessman on the way up (he would one day be politically allied with Julius Caesar) looked around the city for entrepreneurial opportunities.

> **From big needs come big profits**
>
> John D. Rockefeller was arguably the most successful American entrepreneur of all time. Starch-collared, punctilious, rigorously honest, in his youth he worked as an assistant bookkeeper for a produce shipping company in Cleveland, a city with one of the country's few oil refineries. Based on his accounting experience, Rockefeller noted that petroleum-based products like kerosene were shipping with increasing regularity. Putting two and two together, he realized that there were millions of dollars to be made in drilling oil, yes. But there were far fewer risks and just as much profit in refining oil and transporting it. He saw the need, built his own refinery, and the rest is history.

Noting that Rome had no official fire department, Crassus recruited an assortment of laborers, ex-soldiers, and thugs; organized them into crews; equipped them with a fleet of water and hose wagons; and told them to show up wherever a fire broke out. A good idea. Filling a need. But that's not all. Once arrived at the scene of the blaze, the foreman of the crew was to find the owner of the burning building and make him an offer he couldn't refuse: Sell the building at ten percent of its value or the firefighting crew would leave the premises immediately and allow the building to burn to the ground. Needless to say, most owners opted to salvage at least something out of the disaster, and they sold. Crassus was soon the richest man in Rome.

Heartless and criminal? It goes without saying. But still this caper comes down to us from history marked with a sound entrepreneurial principle: Find a basic commercial need in your community and fill it.

Does the city or town you live in (or near) need a good seafood restaurant? A saddle maker? A tax accountant? A resume-writing service? A taxi business? A sporting goods store? A delivery service? If so—and assuming that this particular business is to your liking and that you have some knowledge of it—consider filling the gap.

Look for an entrepreneurial business that is appropriate to the current stage in your life

Chances are if you're over fifty the bloom is off the rose for certain glamorous but physically demanding professions like, say, a DJ at an all-night club, a tap dancer, a skyscraper construction engineer, a professional cyclist.

Not that people over fifty can't do these things. They can. But they usually don't want to. Their workplace skills and preferences have now evolved in different ways. Evolved, for example:

- From take-no-prisoners ambition to satisfaction with a job well done
- From making a lot of money to having enough money
- From taking to giving back
- From apprenticeship to mastery
- From power of body to strength of heart and mind

There are certainly no absolutes in this area. If you want to quit your day job and guide climbers up Mt. Everest, go for it. Broadly speaking though, if you're a member of the fifty-plus generation, choosing a new profession that conforms to the rhythms of your life cycle and maturing world view seems to many a wise and farsighted idea.

Take a potential career for a test drive

Leslie Krasner had worked as a literary agent in New York City for almost thirty years. Extremely successful, she secretly thought she should be working on the other side of the desk, as a writer. At fifty-two she gave up a six-figure salary, along with a host of benefits, and began writing at home.

The problem was that becoming a writer was little more than a romantic idea in Leslie's head. She had done almost no writing in her spare time. She had never taken creative writing courses, never submitted articles for publication, and really, never done much of anything in the field except sell the work of other authors. Result: Within two years, Leslie discovered the painful fact that she was a writer neither by temperament nor talent. When she tried to get her job back at the agency, the doors were closed.

Lesson? Before you take the plunge, get your feet wet.

Of course, it is not always possible to rehearse a job before you do it. But it sure is a good idea to try. If you are thinking of starting a fifty-plus career as a bookbinder, make sure you've logged hours as an apprentice at the trade. If your dream is to become a chef, work part-time in a professional kitchen for a year or two before committing yourself. If you're considering opening a model shop, try selling model planes and cars on the Internet first or working at a hobby store.

Many store owners or service providers will let you work for them at no salary in return for showing you the ropes. Also, spend some time visiting *www.vocationvacations.com*. This site leads you through an "interactive community group experience" (along with a book on the subject) that models the day-to-day realities of certain popular professions. Not perfect, but a passable substitute for the real thing.

Use the VAT assessment tool to help reach your goals

Now that we've hosted you through this inventory of questions and advice concerning fifty-plus entrepreneurship, cap it off by completing the following questionnaire. This Venture Assessment Tool—or easier on the tongue, VAT—is designed to:

- Help you choose the right business for your age and circumstances
- Establish your personal business goals
- Evaluate your business ideas
- Create a plan for establishing your own business

We suggest that you give a few minutes of quality time to use this tool, then ponder your responses. Your answers may surprise you, and, hopefully, answer any lingering questions you have concerning entrepreneurial careers.

Here's the questionnaire.

Venture Assessment Tool (VAT)

1. What Are Your Goals?

The goals that are driving you to establish your new venture will be as individual as you are. Two basic issues to explore are 1) what you want the business to provide you, and 2) how to prioritize your goals.

Here are some goals that people commonly set when starting their own business:

- **Financial goals**—Making money, earning a profit when the business is sold, and garnering benefits such as insurance coverage or tax-deferred pension plans
- **Family goals**—Owning a business that employs relatives and that allows family members to work together
- **Lifestyle goals**—Owning a business that requires a limited time commitment, or that offers personal flexibility, including the opportunity to bring children or grandchildren to work, to enjoy extended vacations, or to work in a field with a strong social or personal agenda such as fitness, health, and education
- **Professional growth goals**—Career development, making use of acquired skills, and the opportunity to face new challenges
- **Social goals**—Carrying out research to cure a disease or providing a service to an underserved group

Following are two VAT worksheets. Both are designed to help you set goals for your new venture. The first worksheet helps you brainstorm your professional objectives. The second asks you to rank your top five choices.

Many aspiring entrepreneurs dream of achieving every goal they set. But realistically speaking, compromises are always necessary and objectives must be balanced one against the other. You cannot, for example, set the goal of working three days a week, then chose a business like a newspaper delivery service or a dairy farm that requires daily participation. Discovering which goals are most important to you and which are secondary is an essential early step in any entrepreneurial venture.

Vat Worksheet for Listing Your Goals
List the following:
- Your financial goals (such as earning current income or building an asset for future sale)
- Your family goals (such as creating business opportunities for family members)
- Your lifestyle goals (such as working part-time or in a specific industry)
- Your professional goals (such as bringing an idea to reality or working in a particular industry)
- Your social goals (such as carrying out research to cure a disease or providing a service to an underserved group)

Next rank the items on this list. These are your basic entrepreneurial priorities.

VAT Worksheet for Ranking Your Top Five Goals

Rank	Goal
1.	
2.	
3.	
4.	
5.	

2. List your skills and expertise—and your weaknesses.
Your next step is to connect your fifty-plus experience, knowledge, skills, and interests to possible fifty-plus-friendly entrepreneurial ventures by filling in the following grid and evaluating your answers.

Personal Inventory and Related Business Skills Worksheet

	Your Response	Businesses that fit well with this strength	Businesses for which this weakness is not a problem
Your primary work experience over the years			
Your areas of greatest knowledge and expertise			
Your strongest skills of any kind			
Your weakest skills of any kind			
Under what specific conditions do you prefer to work? For example, in a team or by yourself			
Your best business or organizational skill			
Your weakest business or organizational skill			
Your major areas of general interest			

3. What is your business idea?

You may have harbored a business notion for years. You may also have developed general ideas that require refinement and development. Now is the time to write it all down. Describe the product or service you hope to provide. Indicate why you think there is an opportunity in this market. Describe who your potential customers are and why they will want to use your particular product or service.

Write Your "Business Idea in a Nutshell" Here

_____
_____
_____
_____
_____
_____
_____
_____
_____
_____

Once you have developed the basic idea for your business, expand on it.

Here is a VAT exercise to help you develop further ideas from your initial concept. On the left-hand column of the Idea Development Grid below are questions. Fill in your responses, adding items in the Variations window if the spirit moves you. The purpose of this exercise is to expand and modify basic concepts in order to improve them. After completing this exercise, decide which variations you like the most and which best suit your personal and financial talents.

VAT Idea Development Grid

Step number	Question	Basic idea	Variations
1.	What is your basic business idea?		
2.	Describe the product or service you wish to sell.		
3.	In which ways could you modify the product or service in order to: A. Give it more status B. Make it less expensive C. Expand the product line D. Fill orders faster E. Find a way to have it patented or copyrighted F. Create a strong brand name		

4.	A. Who or what is the prime market for your product or service? B. Can you modify the product or service to make it appeal to different age, gender, ethnic, and geographical target groups?		
5.	A. How will you package or deliver your product or service? B. How can you make your new product or service more appealing to target markets?		
6.	A. What do similar competitive products or services do differently than the ideas you are proposing? B. Would it make sense to adopt any of their approaches? Which ones?		

4. What is your market?

Once you've developed a new idea from the Idea Development Grid, your next step is to define the market for your business. Answer the following questions:

- Who are your customers? Be specific by age, gender, location, culture, ethnic background, interests, income, and other important characteristics that describe your customer base.
- Why will customers want your product or service? Why might they *not* want your product or service?
- How is your product or service better than those of your competitors?

There are many research tools and data sources to help you learn more about potential markets. Take a look at the Census Bureau website at *www.census.gov* and at the website of the market research firm Claritas which offers definitions of sixty-six market segments at *www.claritas.com/claritas/Default.jsp?ci=3&si=4&pn=prizme_segments*.

5. Is this business a good match for your needs and lifestyle?

Once you have identified your strongest skills and determined if your future business meets your all-around needs, be certain that your skills and talents can help you achieve your goals. If not, you may have to compensate.

Suppose, for instance, that you are a shy person and thus reluctant to approach new people to sell your services. You can overcome this weakness by hiring a sales team that is brimming with charisma and confidence. Filling in the following grid will help you to:

- Define the skills, abilities, and personality characteristics that are required to make your business a success
- Assess your strengths and weaknesses to see if you are well suited to run this business
- Define the gaps between what you already have and what you will soon need
- If necessary, make certain changes to your management to ensure they have all the strengths needed to make your business a success

VAT Worksheet: Making a Match Among Your Venture, Your Team, and You

Possible Needs	Do You Need It?	Do You Have It?	If Not, Where Will You Get It?
Industry knowledge			
Product technical knowledge			
Professional knowledge			
Marketing skills such as knowledge of advertising, PR, and promotion			
Computer knowledge and skills			
Financial skills			
Selling skills			
Management skills			
Social and people skills			
Negotiating skills			
Language skills			
Professional licenses			
Decision-making skills			

Last thoughts on becoming an entrepreneur

A recent AARP bulletin posed some intriguing questions to ask yourself on the topic of fifty-plus entrepreneurship:

- Do you have the energy and drive it takes to start a business after fifty? Is your temperament and personality suited to the task? Ask yourself: Why do I really want to be self-employed? How will self-employment differ from a salaried job? The U.S. Small Business Administration lists the following common reasons for starting an independent business after fifty:

- Become my own boss
- Become more creative
- Gain financial independence
- Draw more fully on my knowledge and skills

To this list AARP adds several final pieces of advice:

- Enjoy freedom for family and recreation
- Keep busy
- Help others
- Have fun

Chapter 3
On the Money: Conventional and Not-So-Conventional Ways to Finance a Business After Fifty

The money issue
The money issue.

The funding dilemma.

The "where will I find the dollars and cents to launch this new business of mine?" question.

Every aspect of a new business revolves around the funding challenge. It's the literal and figurative bottom line. Happily, many studies show that career veterans in their fifties and older are more financially established *and* more economically savvy than their younger competition. As a result, banks and lending institutions are usually friendlier to their loan applications.

But not always.

It's a question of determining the best money sources to tap, knowing the ones you shouldn't waste your time on, and understanding the ground rules for the borrowing game in general.

In this chapter, we will present an insider's tour of the complex mechanics of loan decision-making for small businesses. Credit history, credit scores, personal character assessment, plus personal guarantees and government loan guarantees are all discussed.

We also provide you with methods for determining the risk factors involved in potential businesses. We'll show you how to manage your credit information, and how to access powerful resources at the library or on the Internet.

Finally, we'll examine both conventional and unconventional ways of raising seed money for a business. Included are:

- Credit cards—Should you even *consider* using a credit card to finance a business if you are over fifty? Many people do. But with what results?
- Equity lines of credit.
- Refinancing your home's mortgage—We'll show you how to figure the risks.
- Pension money, savings, IRAs—How safe is this? How sound? In what situations should you *never* dip into personal capital?
- Personal loans from family and friends—Anticipate both the best and the worst on this slippery slope. We provide advice for setting up win-win personal loans.
- Loans from business associates and business connections—You'll need to polish up your persuasive powers if you go this route and perhaps prepare a business plan.
- Angel investors—There are numerous web-based matching services that link up entrepreneurs with independent investors. You are, however, more likely to find the angel of your dreams in a proven professional relationship, such as with a personal accountant or a lawyer who handles your legal dealings. We'll tell you all the best places to seek and find investors.
- Small business grant loans—These are available through several state agencies. There are also private organizations that specialize in business loans for people over sixty. We'll help you find out if you qualify.
- Large companies—Almost impossible if you go in cold. However, if you have an address book full of customers and colleagues you've worked with in the past, and if you are creating a product that suits their needs, they may just be interested.

For the majority of fifty-plus entrepreneurs, high-profile funding sources like venture capital firms or going public are simply not viable options. More realistically, borrowers will find the money they need at banks and institutions or from private lenders.

Banks and independent funding sources do not, of course, lend money to people because they are brave, clean, loyal, and reverent. They lend money because they believe these people can repay said loan—with interest.

This decision, in turn, depends on a strong credit score, a positive business history, and money in the bank. It also depends on clients presenting a lender with a clear, reasonable, and well-thought-out business plan.

Good business plans attract money

After good credit and proof of personal assets, the most important tool you'll need for acquiring a loan is a strong business plan.

What makes a business plan strong?

It would take a book longer than this one you're reading to spell it all out. To give you a nutshell idea, however, it can be said that a strong business plan addresses a potential lender's doubts and goals, and it anticipates and answers a lender's questions before they're asked. Also, using the most relevant facts and figures, it demonstrates in clear, persuasive terms how and why your business will succeed.

A strong business plan must address the specific needs of the lender, whether these needs are evidence of the reasonableness of a business concept, a pledge of prompt payments, proof of financial stability, a guarantee of long-term profits, or simply assurances to a family member who wants you to pursue your dream.

Paula Hornbeck offers a good example of an entrepreneur who used the process of writing a strong business plan as a way to come to terms with the kinds of financing issues that affect people over fifty.

Paula worked for thirty years as a manager of optometrist, optician, and ophthalmologist offices in the Milwaukee area. When it came to the eyeglass business, she had seen it all (no pun intended). In fact, Paula understood so much about the eyeglass world that she often perceived opportunities for improvement that her bosses failed to notice. When she made her suggestions, however, she hit a brick wall. "I got tired of putting good ideas in front of my bosses' noses, only to be shot down every time," she said.

Finally, Paula decided that if she wanted to exploit her business brainstorms and reap the financial rewards, she would have to go entrepreneurial.

As it turned out, Paula had recently married, and her husband, a chemist, was supportive, promising to help her crunch numbers for the business plan. "Even when I saw big problems," Paula said, "my husband kept saying, 'So, why don't you just do it anyway?'"

With her husband's encouragement, Paula signed up for a class in writing business plans at a local college. She soon discovered there was much to learn. "The class started with fifteen people. Only two of us finished."

When she finally wrote her business plan, Paula made it clear to investors that her store would stand out from the others. How? By selling smart, high-design eyeglasses that were unavailable from other stores in the Milwaukee area. She also told potential investors that her store would provide a fun experience for its clients, and that she intended to exploit the selling power of her glamorous products with a glitzy store design. She also included a number of nitty-gritty business elements in the plan: Her intended location, construction fees, a thorough breakdown of rents and salaries, a budget for a designer and a contractor, and an estimate of overall costs.

Paula and her husband had a hefty amount of savings socked away, plus plenty of equity in their home. Her husband also earned a good income. They had no desire to cash in their retirement accounts, nor did they want to sell their house, borrow from friends, or take on partners. Most importantly, they wanted to maintain their lifestyle and to fully own the business themselves.

Paula's business plan eventually convinced a local bank to lend her $200,000 secured by a personal guarantee. Paula and her husband also took $10,000 from their personal savings. This was a canny solution that covered lots of bases, but it was not without risk. A personal guarantee means that if you default on a loan the bank can seize your private assets and sell them. Paula's house and personal savings were now at risk.

At the age of fifty-two, Paula Hornbeck opened her store, Eye Candy Eyewear, in Delafield, Wisconsin. By the third month, she had passed the break-even point. Two years later, working seven days a week, ten to twelve hours a day, she was making a good profit, and loving her business more than ever. The formula for her success was found by mixing thirty years of work experience with a supportive family, a good business plan, and the right kind of financing.

Two types of basic funding you should know about

Debt funding—Debt is an agreement to borrow money and to pay it back on a fixed schedule.

Typically, the repayment plan for a debt includes both interest and principle, principle being the original amount of the loan. In our example, the $200,000 borrowed by Paula represents her principle. Common types of debt include loans, mortgages, lines of credit, borrowing against receivables (i.e., money, goods, or services owed by a customer), and leases.

All professional lenders, be they banks, institutions, or private sources, are avidly concerned with reducing risk of nonrepayment. They therefore require that collateral be put up by a borrower—that is, private assets that a bank can seize and sell if a borrower defaults. Collateral can take the form of equipment, buildings, company stocks, and real estate, including a person's home. Debt with collateral is called "secured debt" and is often required for new ventures.

As a borrower develops a track record for being a successful businessperson and making loan payments on time, lenders become more comfortable increasing the size of their loans and reducing the amount of collateral necessary to secure it. In this regard, many fifty-plus entrepreneurs have an advantage on their side. Older businesspersons tend to have more money in the bank than their younger counterparts. They also have more material assets usable for collateral, and more of a borrowing/repayment history at banks and institutions.

Equity funding—Equity investment grants ownership in a business. It can take the form of stock in a corporation or shares in a partnership. The $10,000 that Paula Hornbeck and her husband invested in their store represents their equity investment.

When investors buy equity, the entrepreneur promises to give them a share of the profits from business operations or from the eventual sale of the company.

Some hardball equity investors require control of the companies they invest in and may demand at least fifty-one percent of the stock. Others are content to be minority shareholders without control. In either case, stock sales in private companies usually involve a contract specifying the precise terms of the investment and the rights of the shareholders. These rights can vary greatly but often include an option to buy more shares or to force the company to buy back the stock within a certain time at a preset price. Creating a shareholders' agreement requires an experienced lawyer who specializes in this area of business law.

Deciding on the balance between debt and equity

Whether debt or equity is preferable for your particular entrepreneurial adventure depends on how much of each your venture can sustain.

Because debt requires that interest and principle be paid on a fixed schedule and that it be paid *right now*—say, the beginning of each month—from the start, your company will be forced to generate enough cash to feed the hungry beast. These mandated payments reduce a company's financial flexibility, yes. But because debt is the least expensive form of financing, usually below ten percent in annual interest, most businesses seek as much of it as they can find. This is why Paula used twenty times more debt than equity to finance her store.

Equity investment, on the other hand, does not require fixed, scheduled payments. This arrangement provides a company with far greater financial flexibility. But it comes at a cost. Because equity investors do not receive financial returns until their debt is paid, they assume greater risk and uncertainty. Ergo, they expect much higher returns in the long run, often at levels two or three times the interest rate on debt. This is why equity investors so often gain control over a company through ownership of shares—often a majority of its shares.

The balance of debt and equity also depends on the track record of the entrepreneur, including business and personal collateral. Remember that Paula was obliged to provide a personal guarantee in order to receive her bank loan. This guarantee meant she had to offer her personal assets as collateral.

In general, investors are most swayed by the attractiveness of the business the entrepreneur is proposing, and by the presence of a clear exit strategy. Example: In a given business plan it states that if the company fails, it will be sold, thus providing lenders with profits despite the fact that the entrepreneur has gone belly-up.

One important question that all fifty-plus entrepreneurs must ask themselves is: "How much should I invest?"

There is no right answer to this question. The tradeoff, as with most financial questions, is one of risk versus reward.

You may, for example, invest as little as possible in a new business to reduce your financial risk (or because you don't have enough money to invest). But this tactic also reduces your share of any eventual profits. On the other hand, you may feel so positive about your company's prospects that you are willing to invest the most money possible. The next section on sources of financing shows that the answer to the risk-versus-reward question involves both a financial *and* a personal decision.

Potential ways to finance your new business

1. The Entrepreneur.

Approximately ninety percent of businesses start with financial investments contributed by the entrepreneurs themselves. Most invest by providing collateral, using credit cards, and/or taking out personal loans.

Now it should be said that no matter how much confidence you may have in the likelihood of success for your new business, the reality is that *many new businesses fail.* You must, therefore, do some serious soul searching. Are you prepared to sell your house, empty your savings, give up your retirement account, or file for personal bankruptcy in case things don't work out as planned?

And going into credit card debt to finance a business is a step that must be considered very, *very* carefully, for obvious reasons. A twenty-two-percent monthly interest rate is no bargain on anybody's books. Moreover, if you are just one day late on your monthly payment, you can sit back and watch your interest rates zip up to over thirty percent in some instances.

Also, have you calculated the interest payment you'll be making on, say, a $9,500 credit card balance at, say, twenty-four percent? Don't even bother. It's a lot of money; so much, in fact, that you'll have to work twenty-four hours a day at your new job simply to pay your tab to Mother Visa/MasterCard and Father American Express.

Many independent fifty-plus entrepreneurs, it should be mentioned, see their venture as just one part of their already established financial situation. They may intend to start the business on a part-time basis, operating other businesses at the same time and opening new ventures when the time is ripe. They may also be focused on a relatively short-term strategy for their businesses, including building it and selling it within a few years.

Many entrepreneurs in this category adopt the "O.P.M." strategy—Other People's Money. They prefer risking as little of their own financial resources as possible while maintaining the flexibility to undertake other ventures. Others see their ventures as a long-term undertaking that they want to control completely without giving half or more to their backers. For the latter group, focusing on the financing they can procure at the lowest possible rate is the best strategy.

2. Family and Friends.

Relatives and close friends are a common source of financing for entrepreneurial ventures. Usually their agendas are more personal than financial. They want to help you succeed.

Some would like to share in your success, and they may see investing in your business as an opportunity to get in on the ground floor. But such goals are usually secondary. Family and friends make good investors for several reasons. They are accessible. You can use your personal relationship with them to encourage their investment. The interest rates they offer, if any, are rarely cutthroat. And if you do get into trouble, most relatives will cut you slack on the monthly payback schedule.

The negative is that if the business fails you must now deal with the "Thanksgiving factor," meaning that during holidays you will be seeing Uncle Martin and Aunt Edith sneering at you across the table. The guilt, oh, the guilt! It was their last $100,000! Can you look them in the eye? Can you ever make things right again?

An early middle-aged entrepreneur named Randy who we met at the entrepreneurial center in Baruch College started a moving company with investments from his parents and father-in-law. On paper it was a good idea. But Randy soon saw the business fail despite all his efforts when the city where he established his company underwent a sudden downturn in the economy.

Randy's parents treated the investment simply as a gift. They told him they thought he had done the best possible job, and that they would invest again if he wanted to start another business. Across the metaphoric Thanksgiving table, however, Randy's father-in-law could never come to terms with his financial loss, and he angrily raised the issue every time they met. Soon, they were barely on speaking terms.

There are several important lessons here. First, be selective about whom you ask for money in the family. Second, be sure to warn your investors of the real financial risks they are taking, and give them every opportunity to say "no." Third, be prepared for long-term negative consequences if your endeavor fails—this is a definite possibility, no matter how thoroughly family investors may have been warned in advance. Nothing ruins relationships, even deep, loving relationships, faster than misunderstandings over money.

All these caveats notwithstanding, family and friends remain a strong potential funding source for most entrepreneurs.

3. Angel Investors.

Angels are wealthy individuals who invest directly in businesses.

Although there are numerous web-based matching services that put potential entrepreneurs in touch with these sources, you are more likely to find one of these heavenly beings through an established personal or business relationship—i.e., via an accountant, perhaps, or a lawyer who handles your business affairs.

Angel investors tend to focus on industries with which they are familiar and with which they have had financial success in the past. Most know the risks involved in investing in a startup or relatively new business. As a result, they tend to expect high returns for their investment. Some will ask for a seat on your board of directors or for an option to purchase enough stock to control the company.

Making a deal with an angel is a bit like getting married. It requires careful thought before the actual commitment is made.

Angel investors who have experience in your industry often have strong ideas about how your business should be run. Unless these ideas closely match your own, this particular marriage may not be the best route. Moreover, when it comes to making deals and talking money, angel investors can be tough, experienced negotiators. They know how important obtaining financing is for you because many have been in the same position. So be prepared for potentially long and complex discussions. Having a lawyer or business consultant by your side during these sessions can be helpful.

4. Venture Capital.

Venture capital firms are generally large, professionally managed funds that invest money that originates from pension funds, large corporations, and/or wealthy individuals. Many are organized as Small Business Investment Corporations (SBICs). This position enables them to obtain Small Business Administration (SBA) guarantees on part of the investments they make in ventures.

Many entrepreneurs think that venture capital is a serious option for them, but in reality, venture capital is a relatively small and highly specialized source of funding. Even in peak years, the venture capital industry makes fewer than 10,000 investments. In most cases, venture capital firms are most comfortable investing several million dollars or more in large private companies that have strong probabilities for growth. Likewise, they prefer to invest in businesses that offer a clear and profitable exit strategy if the company is sold, goes public, or merges with another company. Despite having invested heavily in startups during the dot.com boom, venture capital firms today rarely invest in new businesses.

Another point to note is that when venture capital firms invest in a company, they usually exert as much control over the company as possible. This control gives them many angles of leverage. They can decide what type of financing to obtain. They can decide when and if to sell the business. When push comes to shove, they even have the right to fire the entrepreneur who founded the business in the first place.

When an entrepreneur and a venture capital firm share the same financial agenda, things generally work well. When their goals are different, conflict usually follows. The entrepreneur may feel that the venture capitalists don't have confidence in the long-run prospects of the company, and the venture capitalists may think that making money is not the entrepreneur's main objective.

5. Corporations.

Occasionally, corporations will make direct investments in outside ventures. This situation takes place most frequently in technology industries when a large company such as Intel, for example, invests in a small company that is developing a product Intel desperately needs.

Corporate investments of this type are relatively rare, and almost always carry with them an agreement to sell the company to the corporate investor at some time in the future. It only makes sense, therefore, to consider corporate investors if you have personal contacts at a specific company, if you know for certain that your product is uniquely useful and desirable to that company, and if you feel comfortable with the prospect of losing your independence and becoming at some point a division of the corporation that invests in you.

6. Banks.

Banks usually focus on the financial record and strength of each individual entrepreneur.

In the example of Paula Hornbeck's eyeglass store, the bank exploited Paula's personal financial strength in the form of the personal guarantee that she and her husband provided before they approved the loan. Banks will also look at an entrepreneur's business record, reputation in the industry, and credit score (which is discussed later in this chapter in the section called "How Banks and Other Lenders Decide on Loans").

Banks usually insist that the owner of startup companies back up his or her loans with some form of collateral. Entrepreneurs may be asked to sign a personal guarantee, for instance, or to put up personal assets, including their home. If a company already has a strong record of good credit and high profitability—an unlikely situation in any entrepreneurial startup—or if the company's business assets exceed the amount needed to secure the loan, this personal risk can occasionally be avoided. But this is seldom the case.

Banks tend to be "formula lenders." One formula may, for example, demand a certain percentage of business assets. Others may ask for a multiple of the cash balances that the company maintains in the bank, a multiple of profits, or a multiple of revenue.

Then again, the formula can take the form of a lease. This option is especially attractive to new companies that need heavy-duty equipment and vehicles but that do not have the capital to purchase them.

In a typical lease, the financing firm (usually a bank, but sometimes a commercial leasing or credit company) maintains ownership of the equipment until the lease is fully paid off. If the lease falls into arrears, the leasing company reclaims the equipment. Since the amount of money that changes hands in a lease is relatively small and is extended over a period of time, leases tend to be easier to obtain for entrepreneurs than business loans.

Banks and their rigid lending guidelines frustrate many fifty-plus entrepreneurs. They feel that banks do not "get" the unique financial opportunities their business idea offers, or that the bank's ironclad policies put the kibosh on any real negotiating give and take. What's more, trying to change a particular bank's guidelines is a more or less futile enterprise. A Star Chamber of senior bank officers set these guidelines. A prospective borrower rarely has access to these individuals, and often the loan officers themselves don't know these Star Chamber members' names.

But take heart. Not all banks are the same. Some maintain harsh, unbendable lending policies. Others are more willing to negotiate. A few negotiate a lot. The challenge is to find the reasonable lending organizations and to avoid the inflexible ones. So, shop around. Talk to loan officers at as many banks as possible. Weigh the assets and liabilities of each. Get expert financial advice if it is available. Then take the best deal that comes your way.

7. Going Public.

For most businesses, reaching a position that allows one to go public is the equivalent of winning the lottery.

Look at the numbers. There are more than 10 million businesses in the United States. Only 17,000 are public companies. Of these, 2,800 are traded on the New York Stock Exchange, and 3,300 are traded on the NASDAQ exchange. To be a candidate for a public offering, a company needs around $20 million in annual revenue, plus they must be part of an industry—such as biotechnology or satellite communications—on which Wall Street is currently bullish.

It is, of course, true that during the dot.com boom, many companies with little more than a cute logo were sold to the public. Historically speaking though, that period was an anomaly, and it is now as faint a memory as is much of the money that was so lavishly invested in these soon-to-burst bubbles.

A public company runs on entirely different principles than a private company. Every quarter a public company's performance is held up to the bright light of Wall Street scrutiny. It is the subject of extensive reporting and regulatory requirements and is generally visible to its industry and its competitors.

Public companies, in short, are a world of finance and complexity above the typical entrepreneurial startup. They represent, as it were, the end rather than the beginning of any successful independent business venture. They are definitely *not* a viable alternative for those who are just starting in any given business.

Characteristics of Various Funding Sources

Financing Source	Requires Current Payments?	Requires Share of Profits?	Wants Operating Control?	Cost of Capital
Entrepreneur	No	Yes	Yes	High
Family and Friends	Probably Not	Probably Yes	No	Low
Angel Investors	No	Yes	Input on operations but probably not control	High
Venture Capital	No	Yes	Yes	High
Corporations	Probably Not	No	Eventually, through buyout	High
Banks	Yes	No	No	Low
Public Investors after company goes public	No	Yes	No	Low

Estimating your company's value

Many people, including potential investors, will ask you: "What is your business currently worth?" or a variation on the theme: "How much *will* your business be worth in the future?"

Experienced entrepreneurs reply that their company's value is worth whatever an interested buyer will pay for it. And this is true enough. But business valuations, truth be told, are based mainly on approaches and theories that fit the goals of the purchaser, not the seller. Indeed, investors and lenders will want to know where they stand if the company is sold, or if the company is suddenly shut down. Which means, in turn, that the business plan you use to gain financial backing should include estimates of your company's worth for every year of financial projections that you provide. Typical financial methods of calculating a company's value include the following:

- **Discounted Cash Flow**—This approach relies on estimating profits for the next ten or fifteen years, then calculating the current cash equivalent of this stream of cash inflows (profits) and outflows (investment and losses).
- **Asset Based**—This method focuses on the value of your company's assets, whether they are physical assets such as real estate and equipment, or nonmaterial assets such as patents, customer lists, customer relationships, brand names, and contracts. Lenders will often ask a business to calculate their book value, which is a company's total assets less total liabilities—two numbers that can be found in the financial statements on any good balance sheet. Since assets are likely to have changed in their actual value since they were first recorded on the company's balance sheet, an adjusted book value is sometimes created that is based on the current market value of the company's assets.
- **Replacement Value**—The value of a business can be based on the amount of money it would cost to duplicate that business. For example, replacement value can be applied to a research firm with a strong team of scientists and unique technical systems; or to a restaurant with a well-known name, a good location, and a long-term lease.
- **Liquidation Value**—Liquidation value represents the amount of money a company would produce if it were quickly put up for sale. Liquidation value can include the value of accounts, databases, inventory, physical assets, contracts, leases, and/or the amount of money another company or competitor might pay to purchase the business. The calculation of liquidation

value should account for the costs related to these sales, such as commissions, legal fees, moving expenses, and penalties on leases or contracts.
- **Revenue or Profit Based**—Some industries such as real estate, retail businesses, or the media industry, have relatively well-accepted guidelines for estimating value based on revenue or profits. It is not unusual, for instance, for retail businesses to sell for one or two times their annual revenue. Or for real estate to sell for ten to twenty times profits. Public companies are generally valued at a multiple of their earnings, called the price/earnings ratio. Public companies' shares generally sell in the range of ten to thirty times the earnings per share.
- **Cash Flow/EBITDA Based**—Private companies are often valued at a multiple of cash flow, which in acronym form, EBITDA, stands for Earnings Before Interest, Taxes, Depreciation, and Amortization. This measuring device informs a prospective purchaser of how much cash a company is producing from its operations. And since new owners are not likely to assume the acquired company's outstanding loans, interest and principal payments (amortization) are likely to change after the sale. Depreciation is not a cash item, moreover, so it will reduce profitability on the bottom line of the accounting statements but will *not* have an impact on the amount of cash a company is generating. Taxes are similarly specific to an ownership situation, and to the amount of interest a company is paying. Using EBITDA is a good way to value a private company. It allows prospective owners to decide on the amount and type of financing to obtain, and helps them calculate what their new tax situation will be. Private companies generally sell in the range of three to ten times cash flow or EBITDA.

Creating financial models

Because your projections represent the heart of the business plan you show to potential funding sources, it is critical that you work with a high quality financial model that combines all the financial aspects of your venture into one. Financial models are usually produced via a spreadsheet program that allows numbers to be linked. In this way, a change made to one figure automatically generates changes to projected statements and analyses.

Creating a model from scratch is an excellent exercise. It forces you to consider all the financial assumptions in your business plan. It also shows you how well—or poorly—the model works, allowing you to make changes where appropriate. There are several readily available spreadsheet tools that can help in this regard:

- *www.bankablebusinessplans.com* has many resources, including sample spreadsheets you can review and download.
- One of the best spreadsheet models is Active Ventures produced by the Columbus Enterprise Development Corporation. It is comprehensive, all the tables are linked, and it is free. It is available at: *www.cedcorp.com.*
- An easy-to-use financial projection model is available on the Missouri SBDC website: *http://www.missouribusiness.net/docs/crunching_numbers_projections.asp.* Produced by Aldis Jakubovskis, this model is simple, yet it clearly shows which assumptions have to be entered. It also produces completed projected statements based on these assumptions.
- Commerce Clearing House (CCH) has a very useful site for entrepreneurs at *www.toolkit.cch.com.* It has model spreadsheets, as well as useful and up-to-date tax-planning tools.
- Many quality sample business plans are available on websites for business plan competitions such as the MOOT Corporation competition at the University of Texas, at *www.businessplan.org.*
- Excel templates are available with the CD that accompanies the *MBA's Guide to Microsoft Excel 2002* by Stephen L. Nelson, published by Redmond Technology Press.

If you intend to build your financial model from scratch, or to modify an existing one, there are several helpful guidelines to follow:

- Examine your finished model *in detail*. It is not sufficient to review the model to see if it "looks" correct. Test it by proofreading carefully and by checking all spreadsheet cell references and formulas.
- Test the model by making changes to assumptions and checking to see if these changes flow through the rest of the model.

- Compare the model to others from similar companies to ensure that it uses standard industry categories.
- Have accountants, financial professionals, or people with industry experience review the model.

How banks and other lenders decide on loans

Every time banks, equipment leasing companies, commercial credit companies, and credit card companies make a loan, they assume a risk that they will not be paid back. They manage this gamble in a number of ways:
1. By lending to low-risk people whom they deem creditworthy;
2. By lending less than the customer is requesting;
3. By exacting a guarantee from a third party whom they judge to be creditworthy;
4. By charging higher interest rates and fees to compensate for accepting the risk;
5. By obtaining collateral to seize and sell if the loan is not paid back; and, most often,
6. By not lending at all.

What's more, loan decisions at a lending or business institution are made on the grounds of personal factors, including all of the following:

- **Credit history**—In this electronic age, lending sources can instantly evaluate how quickly you have paid your bills and how thoroughly you have fulfilled your obligations to banks and other financial companies. Information on late payments, delinquent loans, and bankruptcies, as well as how much credit has been extended to you in the past by banks, credit card companies, department stores, and credit bureaus is readily available to potential financial sources at the touch of a few computer keys.
- **Character**—A loan decision will often come down to a personal evaluation of the borrower made by one or more loan officers. Sometimes financing may be denied to people with stellar credit histories because the loan officer's sixth sense is triggered. At other times—though rarely—lenders will grant loans to entrepreneurs of exemplary character who show very low credit scores or even bankruptcies in their past. A loan

made to a person with low credit worthiness is called a *"character loan."* A bank may make such a character loan to meet its internal guidelines for lending within certain geographic areas or because the bank is truly impressed with the novice entrepreneur.

- **Collateral**—Houses financed by them collateralize mortgages. The equipment being leased collateralizes the lease. Collateral assures banks they will be paid back if loan payments are in arrears or if the business defaults on the loan. Most lending sources require existing collateral, such as an entrepreneur's house, securities, or other assets, before they will grant a small business loan.
- **Personal guarantee**—Lending sources go to great lengths to make sure that entrepreneurs are liable for their loans. Personal guarantees provide this assurance. If you own a home with significant equity value, or if you maintain a large savings or investment account, giving the bank a personal guarantee on these items will make the officers very happy—just as it should make *you* very nervous.
- **Government loan guarantees**—Federal agencies, such as the Small Business Administration (SBA) and various state programs help banks say "yes" to loans by agreeing to guarantee repayment of some portion of the loan in case of default, ranging between fifty percent and ninety percent. While these government loan guarantees carry a paperwork burden for both the entrepreneur and the lender, they encourage lenders to feel more comfortable approving a loan. Going this route offers an excellent option to banks for several reasons:
    - Banks often obtain government guarantees on loans they would have made without the guarantee. This increases the safety of the loan without reducing its profitability.
    - Banks can "bundle" and sell the guaranteed portion of these loans to larger financing companies or on the public bond market, thus earning an immediate profit.
    - Banks receive credit with bank regulators for making SBA-guaranteed loans. This credit helps the bank remain in good standing with the government regulators.

The presence of a government guarantee rarely stops a lender from asking for—and usually receiving—other collateral or personal guarantees for the loan. This gives bankers more than 100% in collateral and guarantees and is rather like wearing both a belt and suspenders—unnecessary and unattractive, but they certainly keep your pants up.

- **Credit Scoring**—Some credit research firms, most notably Fair, Isaac, and Company—now FICO®, calculate a single figure, which they call a *credit score*. Factors used in determining this figure include your payment history, the amount of your borrowing relative to your credit lines, recent inquiries made by other financial institutions, and the types of credit you most frequently use.

All these are then put into a computer model that then produces a single number. This number is scored on a scale that begins at 400, the lowest possible credit rating, all the way up to 900, which represents that illusive pie in the sky, "perfect credit." Although there is no single credit score number that banks require, most prefer a credit score of 680 or higher before they say yes to loaning anyone money.

A *credit report* lists the history of all your financial activity. It is different from a credit score that pulls all this information together and calculates a single number. Credit reports and scores are produced by three main credit-ratings companies: Transamerica, Equifax, and Experian. You can check your credit report with the credit-ratings companies directly, or go to *www.myfico.com* and for about forty-five dollars purchase your credit reports and the scores from all three credit-ratings companies. There is also a nationwide system in the United States currently being rolled out state by state that will enable individuals to obtain their credit scores from the credit-ratings companies at no charge once a year.

Finally, for any banker, the best loan is one in which the business generates enough money to make interest payments comfortably, and to eventually return all the bank's money. When a company performs as anticipated, meets its obligations, and even grows to the point that its credit needs increase, the bank, the loan officers, and the entrepreneur have a win-win situation on which they can build a long-term, mutually beneficial business relationship.

This long-range, productive business relationship must start with financial projections that bankers find credible, and which then *prove* to be credible. A strong credit score, showing yourself to be of good character, and providing quality collateral or guarantees are all well and good. But in the end, the thing that banks like to see most is the prospect that your new company will be a strong and steady earner for many years to come.

Chapter 4
What Every Entrepreneur Hates: Legal Issues, Boards of Directors, Insurance, and Taxes

Defense, defense, defense

Muhammad Ali, one of the greatest boxers and perhaps the greatest *defensive* boxer of all time, said, "He who is not courageous enough to take risks will accomplish nothing in life."

But Ali also knew how to minimize his risks. His basic strategy in the ring was to keep moving backward defensively until he saw an opening that allowed him to unleash his powerful offense. Whether in sports or in business, sometimes you have to play defense as well as offense. And fifty-plus entrepreneurs need to play defense exceptionally well.

Think about what happened with the financial crisis of 2008 and 2009.

Virtually everyone was hurt to a degree by the drop in value of homes and investments, but some people were hurt much more than others.

There doesn't have to be a collapse of the worldwide financial markets for anyone to be battered by the IRS. Poor planning, missed filings, and mistakes in choosing the best legal structure for tax purposes can give the IRS an opening that they will use to knock out any entrepreneur. Disgruntled partners can turn board meetings into brawls and business issues into messy, expensive, and time-consuming lawsuits. Creditors, especially those who are extra nervous in a downturn, are always ready to floor you with a flurry of lawsuits. Lack of proper insurance when disaster strikes will put any business down for the count.

If you make any of these or myriad other critical business blunders, aggressive lawyers will be more than happy to turn your company—and your life—into nonstop misery. For entrepreneurs who start a new business in later life and who put their reputations and hard-earned finances on the line, these events can be devastating. If you get KO'd by any of these, there may not be any rematches.

This chapter will show you how to build the proper defenses into your fifty-plus entrepreneurial business at the beginning so you will be protected from the worst-case scenarios that cost you money, close your business, and break your heart. Building these defenses requires knowledge of company organization, legal issues, financial risks, insurance, and taxes, *plus* strategic planning, *plus* awareness that financial and organizational issues are often different for aspiring businesspersons over fifty than they are for their younger competition.

Let's begin by reflecting on the case a fifty-two-year-old experienced businessperson I'll call Robert Deleuze. Robert had a great business idea but the wrong investors and board members. As a result, his growing venture turned into an ugly mess. His story shows the importance of choosing the right people around you whether they are in the role of advisors, directors, investors, or partners.

Robert is a brilliant, energetic, and creative entrepreneur who in midlife founded a chain of nationally franchised fast food stores that I'll call Foodtopia. His reputation, his innovative business ideas, and his established financial credentials helped him attract financing from banks, suppliers, private investors, and venture capital firms. He opened his first few stores to much acclaim. Robert was interviewed in national magazines, and appeared on the business segments of network television news and talk shows. He recruited a board of directors who invested money in the business and who believed that Foodtopia would sweep the nation and make all its investors—especially them—into multimillionaires.

Robert was incredibly busy. He was constantly raising money for Foodtopia because, like most growing companies, Foodtopia required regular infusions of fresh capital to sustain its growth. Setting up a franchise system required nearly a million dollars in legal and marketing fees, and corporate staff had to be hired even before there were profits to support them. Each new store cost about $500,000 just to open. Robert was also the person primarily responsible for building the systems to operate the stores. Questions such as what the signs would look like, what cash register system would be used, and what the hours of operation would be were among the hundreds that Robert had to answer.

Robert was under so much pressure to raise more and more capital that he paid little attention to his lawyer's advice to be careful in choosing his investors. His lawyer had seen this movie before: The entrepreneur has long-term plans to build the business while the investors want fast returns and couldn't care less if the business realizes the entrepreneur's vision. The investors had also seen the movie and knew to demand seats on the board of directors so that—at a time of their choosing—they could dictate what happens to Foodtopia.

Because of overwhelming interest from prospective franchisees, international food companies, and the media, Robert and his investors never had a moment's doubt that in a short time their investments would be paid back many times over.

But things did not go as planned.

Foodtopia was spending more on store openings and selling franchises than it was making in profits from its first few stores. The company began to experience cash flow problems as a result.

Foodtopia also started paying its bills late, even its insurance and tax bills. Revenues were lower than projected, and expenses were higher. Soon their losses mounted, generating a need for more infusions of cash.

Compounding problems, board members became impatient, blaming Robert for the slowdown and demanding that he raise more money or find investors to buy them out.

Meanwhile, the bank saw the company foundering financially and stopped lending Robert money. Seeing the writing on the wall, Robert found a large international fast food company that wanted to buy Foodtopia. But the investors and board members still had hopes of becoming rich and rejected the offer because they did not feel the price was high enough.

Now the real downward spiral began.

The bank called in its loans and would not let Robert withdraw money even from his personal account. Suppliers heard about the company's financial woes and demanded payment up front for everything from milk to napkins. If Foodtopia didn't pay in advance, the supply pipeline would shut down entirely.

In the end, not even the board members got their wish.

They didn't get the huge price for the company that they hoped for, and Foodtopia was sold to a large fast food company for a fraction of its value and, notably, a fraction of the offer Robert had negotiated previously and which the board had turned down. None of the company's original lenders was paid back, and investors received nothing. Robert, meanwhile, was left with a mountain of personal debt because of money he personally had invested. He considered declaring bankruptcy but did not want this blot on his business record. Today he is still paying off his debt.

Robert's story shows how certain key decisions such as choosing your partners and investors made during optimistic times cannot be undone during bad times. His story shows the importance of building a strong support team from the start. Robert's board members were more interested in making decisions that benefited themselves first and placed Robert and the company last. Suppliers and lenders were eager to join what they hoped would be the next McDonald's or Starbucks, but they quickly backed away when they began to perceive the downside risks growing. The company's lawyers and Robert's personal lawyers began to demand upfront payment. So you can see how Robert was knocked to the canvas without nary a helping hand to get up again.

This chapter explains how to prevent this and other bad outcomes from becoming your story.

Entrepreneurship is a team sport—so build the right team

In the final analysis, Robert's main problem was the lack of a good team around him.

He had one partner and a few advisors who always put the company's and Robert's interest's first. But just about everyone else was only looking for immediate personal gain.

Of course, businesses are fundamentally about making money, and it is hardly unreasonable for suppliers, accountants, or employees to stop working for you when they can't be paid. But you also need people who will support you through good times and bad without expecting to be paid every week or earn millions from stock options in the near future.

You can organize a board of directors, which is required by law for a corporation, or you can form a board of advisors, a group without any formal legal role whose job is simply to advise you and your company. When businesses succeed, it is not uncommon or unreasonable for directors and advisors to share in that success through stock ownership or contracts with the business for services they can supply. If you select the right people and make the expectations clear, you will build a team around you that will take a long-term view of your business and be there to help you achieve your long-range goals.

Boards of directors have an ultimate and legal responsibility for the actions taken by a corporation. Directors have legally defined roles, responsibilities—and liabilities.

Carrying directors and officers insurance can minimize these liabilities, but many people are still reluctant to be directors out of fear of being pulled into messy company lawsuits.

In addition to being insured, many prospective directors want to be paid in fees or stock or both. These fees give them a current income for their work, and the stock brings the promise of future gains if the company grows. Because a board of advisors is an informal group, it has no legal authority over the company, and its members have no personal liability for any actions the company takes. As a result, it is generally easier to recruit people to be on a board of advisors than a board of directors.

Both directors and advisors should be chosen for their industry experience, financial background, and technical understanding. A high-powered, capable, and contributing group of directors or advisors will:
- Make your business (or your business plan if you haven't started yet) especially attractive to potential investors or lenders;
- Help you make the right decisions in operating and financing the business;
- Add their own business contacts to yours to help you raise capital, obtain clients, and find the best suppliers and partners; and
- Provide technical expertise based on their knowledge and experience.

For each potential board of directors or board of advisors member, you should complete the following template:

Worksheet for Building a Board of Directors or a Board of Advisors

Step 1. Fill in the following table to identify the expertise and connections that will be especially valuable to your business.

Categories of Positives that Members of the Board of Directors or Board of Advisors Can Deliver	Particular People Who Can Bring These to Your Board	Specifics of How Each Individual Will Provide These
Specialized knowledge, such as particular skills, languages, degrees, and certifications.		
Membership in organizations such as professional societies, local business groups, country clubs, and fraternal associations. These contacts will bring access to potential customers, investors, or providers of resources your business needs.		
Connections to major customers, investors, possible purchasers of your business (or sellers of companies you would like to buy), or major suppliers that could help your business accomplish its goals more quickly and effectively.		
Experience with companies or industries similar to your own which can help you make the best decisions and avoid the worst mistakes.		
A blend of personality types who are cautious, aggressive, upbeat, or motivators and who can help your board of advisors and your company run more effectively.		

Step 2. Rank the people listed in the center column in order of those who will offer the most to your business right now.

Step 3. Develop a plan for contacting potential board members. You may know some people personally and others may come through friends or colleagues. If you have no personal connection with these prospects, write a letter, send an email, or call to introduce yourself and your idea. The majority of these people will be flattered by your interest, will probably want to help, and may even say yes right away without putting you through too much interrogation. For those who are less gracious, all you can do in such cases is resolve never to treat others in this way, and move on to the next person on your list.

Step 4. Keep in frequent touch with board members through email, telephone calls, and meetings. Hold full meetings three or four times per year at convenient times and places. Make each meeting a productive working session by establishing an agenda and placing questions you are pondering on the table for board comment. Discuss specific company needs and identify board members who can help you fill them.

Hiring the right employees

Hiring and retaining the right employees is fundamental to your company's success, so establish your approach and strategy to such key functions as compensation, insurance, training, and management from the start. Within large companies, this area is called human resources. For your new or smaller business, this is a sector you will manage yourself.

Of course, not all the things that large companies do, such as retirement plans or training programs, will apply to you. But it is something you must make decisions about from the beginning of your business, or even earlier, when you are writing your business plan.

Robert hired people for the corporate office and to manage stores who had industry experience and knowledge. Most of them didn't share his enthusiasm for the business concept but wanted to be part of a fast-growing business in which they could make big money quickly. When the company hit bumps in the road, their lack of long-term commitment to the company caused them to lose interest, and many left, hurting Foodtopia's reputation with suppliers and funders. Here are some of the issues you'll need to consider:

- **Identify key positions**—Since business is a team sport, choosing your teammates may be the most important decision you'll make. It's useful to fill out the grid below for every key position in your organization. A summary of this information can go in your business plan or be used as a guide to hire people.

Information Required for Key Positions

Title of the position	
Job description	
Required degrees, training, and/or experience for the person who will fill the position	
Compensation including salary, bonuses, stock ownership, and stock incentives	
The employee's résumé if the position is currently filled	
The résumé of someone you have in mind for the position	
How you will conduct the search for the position if necessary	

- **Employee compensation and benefit plans**—The compensation and benefits package you offer employees should fit your overall business strategy.

If you are opening a fast food franchise, your employees will consist mainly of people under age twenty-five. Most of these young men and women will think of their jobs less as long-term careers and more as a way to earn cash in the short run to pay for school or buy a car.

For such young cohorts, a compensation plan that maximizes their paychecks at the expense of long-term benefits (such as pension plans) is probably best.

On the other hand, if you are developing a consulting firm and need committed employees to build strong, ongoing relationships with your clients, a plan that stresses long-term benefits such as health insurance, stock ownership, or pensions is best.

Employee benefits is a very complex, highly regulated, rapidly changing area. You should consult with a benefits company or a financial planner and receive actual proposals for employee benefits.

- **Principal suppliers and contractors**—Henry Ford's first automobile plant functioned by funneling coal, iron ore, and other raw materials in one door of the factory and rolling finished Model Ts, fresh off the assembly line, out the other door. When Ford began his business, no one was manufacturing and supplying car parts. His factory had to do it all. In today's world, most companies subcontract out large portions of their essential processes. Dell assembles computers from components it purchases from hundreds of different suppliers. Toyota requires its suppliers to locate their facilities adjacent to the Toyota plants so parts can be ordered and delivered within a few hours.

Chances are that your venture will follow Dell's or Toyota's model of outsourcing more than Henry Ford's, which means that you will need to identify and assemble a list of proposed suppliers. Here are some questions about suppliers that you should answer:

- What materials will they be supplying?
- How long have they been in business?
- What are their credentials and track records?
- Why have you selected these companies in particular? Price? Quality? Ability to supply the adequate quantity on time?
- Have they made a binding offer to supply certain products or services at a definite price?
- What is your backup plan if the supply company does not fulfill its obligations?

Suppliers with strong track records and excellent reputations will contribute quality materials to your business. Because so many products follow a supply chain that moves from process to process, company to company, and even country to country, the competitiveness of your final product will depend on your ability to manage this movement along a supply chain. Maybe you're thinking that this doesn't apply to you, but it actually applies to almost every business. Perhaps you want to be a consultant and use a blog to communicate with your potential or current clients. Perhaps you want to buy and sell antiques either through a store or online, or both. You'll have a supply chain, too. In these examples, the company that hosts your blog, sells you the antiques that you then market, or ships the antiques to your customers is part of the deal as well.

Supply chain management requires that you choose the right supplier who provides the right service reliably and at the right price, along with usable information to help you run your business.

For example, website hosting companies offer data on where your site's visitors are coming from and how they are using your website. For products with physical inventories, software tracks inventory levels, anticipates future needs, reports a supplier's inventory levels and, given normal shipping times, projects time schedules for shipments.

Guidance for using lawyers and accountants.

As an older entrepreneur, you probably have already dealt with lawyers and accountants a number of times in your life. So perhaps what I am about to tell you is old news.

Whatever the case, it's always a wise idea to consult them *but* not to let them make so many of your major decisions that they end up running your business. These professionals, no matter how experienced and well meaning, cannot really understand your business and your vision as well as you do. Decisions such as legal structure, key contracts, or finance all require your leadership.

Sometimes when starting a business it's better to *not* delegate.

Options for legal structure.

Many entrepreneurs find choosing a legal structure for their company a daunting prospect. Some entrepreneurs simply start doing business without any legal structure in place at all. They have clients who just write out checks to them. They purchase items needed to start their business on their personal credit cards. They order a personal residential phone. By doing this, they build a strong case for the IRS to tax their business profits as personal income, and for a disgruntled employee or customer to sue them personally.

Don't make this mistake. Go legal.

All you need to do is pick the right legal structure. Now I know that some people don't like to file papers with the IRS or with their state, but doing this is nonetheless the best and safest way to go. Whether or not you hire a lawyer or accountant to help you through this process, understanding your choice of legal structures is a good idea and, in fact, may not be as complicated as you think. These legal tax structures come in a variety of forms including the following:

- **Sole Proprietorships**—These have one owner who manages the business and contributes to the investment. There is no liability protection with sole proprietorships, and profits and losses are passed through directly to the owner's tax return.
- **General Partnerships**—These can have as many partners as desired, all of whom are collectively responsible for managing the business, and all of whom contribute to the investment and share in the profits. There is no liability protection offered in this arrangement, and profits and losses pass through directly to each partner's individual tax return.
- **Limited Partnerships**—This structure features two classes of partners: The general partners who are responsible for the management of the business, and the limited partners who are simply investors. (General partners can also invest as limited partners.) Based on the profit-sharing agreement between the two classes of partners, profits and losses pass through to both the general and limited partners' individual tax returns. General partners have no personal liability protection. Limited partners do.
- **S Corporation**—This structure is taxed like a partnership, but it provides the liability protection of a corporation. It also allows profits and losses to pass through to the shareholders. There are some restrictions on this deal, including that: 1) the number of shareholders is fewer than

seventy-five; 2) that there is only one class of stock; and 3) all shares are owned by certain types of shareholders such as individuals, trusts, or estates.
- **C Corporations**—C Corporations are usually the structure of choice for large companies. They allow for an unlimited number of shareholders and for an unlimited number of classes of stock. Shareholders have no personal liability, and a board of directors, which in certain cases can be held liable for the company's actions, manages the company. The C Corporation also pays taxes on its profits. These profits pass through to the shareholders in the form of dividends, which are then taxed again on the individual shareholders' tax returns.
- **Limited Liability Companies**—These allow for an unlimited number of investors, called members. The owners can elect to let profits and losses pass through to the members' individual tax returns or be taxed at the corporate level. Members of this type of corporation cannot be held liable for actions of the company.
- **Limited Liability Partnerships and Professional Corporations**—These are state-sanctioned organizational forms designed for licensed professionals such as lawyers, accountants, doctors, and dentists. If you are starting a business as a member of such a profession, you should ask an attorney who specializes in serving your particular profession about the advantages of using one of these forms.

There are three major concerns to consider when in choosing a legal structure for your venture:
1. **Tax considerations**—Certain structures, such as limited partnerships, do not pay taxes directly. Instead, they pass profits and losses directly through to their owners. The owners then pay taxes based on their own particular tax situation.
2. **Liability considerations**—Some legal entities, such as corporations, protect their owners from liabilities resulting from missteps by the company or its employees through what is known as the "corporate veil." This protection is not perfect, and in cases of fraud or illegal activity, the corporate veil can be pierced.

3. **Investor considerations**—The type, number, and wealth of investors involved in your venture are all important due to the fact that some structures are hemmed in by certain restrictions. An S Corporation, for instance, limits the number of possible investors. General partnerships have only one class of investors. C Corporations allow for many. The option of having more than one class of investors means that you can give varying voting or economic power to different groups of investors. Note that government reporting requirements are different for companies that only raise money from professional investment groups and wealthy individuals. Once you analyze these considerations, you can match your needs with the types of legal entities available, and then make the best choice. The following table shows how to match these three considerations with the legal form that is best for your company:

Choices for Legal Entities

Form	Number of Shareholders/ Partners	Personal Liability	Taxed at Company's Level or on Owner's Taxes
Sole Proprietorship	One	Yes	Owner's
General Partnership	Many	Yes	Owner's
Limited Partnership	Many	No	Owner's
S Corporation	Up to seventy-five	No	Owner's
C Corporation	Many	No	Company's
Limited Liability Company	Many	No	Owner's
Limited Liability Partnership	Many	No	Owner's
Professional Corporation	One	Yes	Owner's

The question of health insurance.
There are no legal requirements to provide health insurance for employees in this country.

However, you may still want to provide it for yourself and your employees. Managing health insurance can, of course, be about as complicated as decoding the human genome. Members of the fifty-plus generation remember when insurance cost a family less than $100 a month, and you were free to choose your own doctors. The self-serving logic and arbitrary rules that health care plans have now shackled the American public and drive just about everyone crazy with their endless delays, paperwork, and fine print. At the same time, we also know that it is best for you and your employees to be properly insured.

Most companies use an insurance agent who shops for and helps manage the health insurance plan. If you decide to use an agent, make certain that he or she works with more than one or two select insurance companies, and that you are offered a wide range of costs and programs.

Know, too, that most health insurance rules are set by your state, which means that the structure and quality of insurance plans are heavily affected by the geographic location of your company. Keeping in mind that rules vary by state, here are your basic health insurance options as a fifty-plus entrepreneur:

- **Do nothing**—You are not legally obliged to insure your employees. This is a good idea if you have insurance coverage from another source (such as Medicare with a wraparound policy), but it's a bad idea if you don't. People do, after all, get sick.
- **Buy a company policy**—There are policies for companies with as few as two employees, and you can share these costs with employees in any way you wish. Such policies can be traditional insurance that pays specified amounts for medical care. They can be HMOs (Health Maintenance Organizations), or they can be PPOs (Preferred Provider Organizations), which require use of in-network providers.
- **Establish medical savings accounts**—This system allows you to put pretax dollars into an account for each employee. The employees can then use this money for medical expenses without paying income tax on it.

You, older workers, and Medicare.
People over sixty-five are eligible for Medicare as provided by the federal government. Overall, it is good health coverage. Some fifty-plus employers even make a point of hiring workers over sixty-five so that Medicare obviates the need for any group health insurance.

However, Medicare only covers a certain percent of medical costs. To be fully insured, a Medicare supplement or wraparound policy is needed, and, perhaps not surprisingly, these are not that much cheaper than insuring a non-Medicare-covered employee.

In any event, you will need to shop for Medicare supplements just as intensively as you would for regular insurance. Expect a time-consuming, brain-rattling process. But be of good cheer, as there are affordable and effective Medicare supplements are out there. You just have to look extra hard.

Business insurance.
Some business insurance is required and some is optional. Both are expenses most entrepreneurs would rather forego.

We sympathize, but the fact is if you fail to purchase the right type of insurance, you place both your business and personal assets at risk. One lawsuit, one liability case, one flood, and you can lose it all.

Here are the types of business insurance you are most likely to need:

- **Workers' compensation**—This pays medical bills and lost wages for employees if they are injured on the job. It is required by every state in the Union. Actual rates are set on a state-by-state basis. After you've been in business for a while, your company will have its rate set based on how many claims have been filed.
- **General liability**—This type of insurance protects you if someone is injured on your premises, or if someone is injured by one of your products.
- **Property and casualty**—This insurance protects the physical assets of your business from risks such as fire, theft, and flood.
- **Auto insurance**—This is necessary if your business has vehicles, unnecessary if it doesn't.
- **Directors and officers liability**—This policy provides personal coverage to members of the board of directors and officers of

your company if they are sued personally because of some action of the company.
- **Umbrella policies**—These will provide coverage above the specifics of other liability insurance in case your losses exceed the maximums on those other policies.
- **Business-interruption insurance**—This replaces lost income in the event that your business cannot operate due to catastrophic weather, lost power, or lack of phone service, subject to the specific terms of the policy you buy.
- **Life insurance**—This is carried by many business owners as a way to give financial support to their families after they die, but many lenders and investors will also require a form of life insurance, called *key-person insurance,* which provides funds to the business in the event of the death of an essential principal or employee.
- **Disability insurance**—This policy provides income replacement in the event of a long-term illness. Disability insurance usually has a short-term benefit (from a few months to a year) and a long-term component (longer than a year). You also need to pay attention to the waiting period until benefits begin.

State and city permits, filings, and—yes—taxes

The federal government is not the only level of government you need to worry about. States, cities, and counties all may have something to say about your business, require you to have permits and pay fees, and tax you and your business. Failing to comply can have dire consequences such as your business being shut down and charged huge penalties. Every locality is different, but, generally speaking, here is what you need to look for:
- **Permits and licenses**—You can't open a liquor store, have a taxicab service, sell food, or hang an outdoor sign in most places without permits and licenses. In California, you can't hang wallpaper without a license. In Louisiana, you can't be a florist without passing an exam and obtaining a license. In West Virginia, you need a license to install carpet. So be careful! Research local issues before you start and make sure you are properly licensed.

- **Registering your name**—In many states and localities, you need to register (and pay for) any name other than your own legal name. So if you are a sole proprietor but do business as Speedy Computer Repair, you need to register this legal name. This business name is called your DBA or Doing-Business-As name.
- **Get ready for inspections**—Once you open your business, you may be subject to inspection by agencies such as the Fire Department or the Environmental Control Board of your locality. They have rules about exits, fire extinguishers, storage of chemicals, discharging waste, and doing business in residentially zoned areas. Be ready!
- **State and local taxes**—Sales taxes, real estate occupancy taxes, and business registration fees are just a few of the many state and local taxes that your government will be eager to collect from you. Research what they are on your own or rely on your accountant to help you.
- **Payroll taxes**—When you have employees, you need to be registered with the IRS by obtaining an Employer Identification Number or EIN. This takes about five minutes and can be done over the phone or online. Then you need to withhold FICA (Federal Insurance Contributions Act) taxes that cover Social Security and Medicare. You also will pay FUTA (Federal Unemployment Tax Act) taxes, which go into the system that pays unemployment insurance. This money is remitted to the IRS electronically or paid by check on a monthly or quarterly basis. And yes, there is even more—more than we can cover here—including state and local taxes. Most businesses use an accountant or an automated payroll system. But the key thing to know is that failure to pay or pay on time results in heavy penalties.
- **Immigration rules**—Employers need to verify that every employee has valid immigration status at the time of hiring by filing an I-9 form. Penalties for failure to follow these rules are huge, and may include going to jail. It is hard to operate your business from jail, so pay attention to this!
- **Occupational Safety and Health Administration (OSHA) rules**—Every business of any size and in any industry is

covered by OSHA rules. These are specially designed to reduce the risk of serious injury and death in the workplace. They run the gamut from first aid procedures to specialized regulations for virtually every industry. OSHA is part of the Department of Labor, and its rules and regulations are available at *www.osha.gov*. It may not be much fun, but you should plan on spending some time doing research on this website to see which rules will apply to you. You can also ask your insurance company for guidance.
- **Antidiscrimination laws**—In companies with fifteen or more employees, civil rights laws prevent discrimination based on race, ethnicity, gender, disability, or religion. These laws apply to the hiring, promotion, and compensation of employees. If one of your employees is accused of discrimination, you and your business can be sued. These require you to make antidiscrimination a policy that you implement by educating and managing your employees.
- **Sexual harassment laws**—Federal laws also protect employees from being sexually harassed in the workplace. The rules are complex and what constitutes harassment is often based on what makes an individual feel uncomfortable. So here again, educating yourself and your employees is the way to go.

The crying towel

So are you really depressed yet?

Don't be.

Every successful business has navigated these dangerous waters, and you can, too. There is a great deal to learn, but there are many tools you can use to minimize the impact on your time so that you can focus on building your business.

Good luck.

Chapter 5

Your Personal Work-at-Home Handbook

Escaping the downtown office blues
So here it is, the big one. The longtime impossible dream shared by an army of aspiring entrepreneurs, all fifty-plus, most of whom by now have had their fill of grumpy bosses, claustrophobic office cubicles, and one day off for Christmas.

Year after year, these work warriors have spent their nine-to-fives lunching at greasy spoon restaurants, at death star company cafeterias, and even out of paper bags. They have dragged their tired bodies home every night at nine or ten o'clock. They have side-stepped lecherous colleagues, fought off sleep at endless staff meetings, put up for years with those lovable folks upstairs in accounting. And finally, at the end of the day, when the time comes to take inventory, many have made a jarring discovery: one-twelfth of their waking lives have been spent commuting to and from the office.

The soldiers in this vast and weary army are ready, very, VERY ready to quit their day jobs, and spend the rest of their lives working at a business they can own and operate at home.

"If I work at home in my own domestic setting," an about-to-retire clothing salesperson named Niles recently told me, "this will improve on just about everything that made life on the [sales] floor such a pain. It will give me my freedom, it's a decent living, there'll be time to visit with my girlfriend, some mobility, more time to travel around the country, see friends, be my own boss, and get some peace and quiet while I work."

Whether or not such a rosy ideal of home office life is entirely accurate, partially accurate, or not accurate at all, we will find out as the chapter unfolds. At this point, we can say simply that it *is* accurate—with qualifications. Beware: Some of them are serious qualifications.

Kurt Thometz is one of those weary soldiers. Born in St. Cloud, Minnesota, as a young man he worked at the Guthrie Theater in Minneapolis. This experience introduced him to great writing and gave him a taste for the literary life.

In 1972, Kurt moved to New York City where he first worked at the legendary Strand Bookstore, then at the Madison Avenue Bookstore located in the center of the very upscale East Side of Manhattan.

One of Kurt's customers at the Madison Avenue Bookstore was the legendary Diana Vreeland, former editor of *Harper's Bazaar* and *Vogue* magazines, and then curator of the Metropolitan Museum of Art's costume collection. Over time, the two book lovers developed a friendship (Vreeland would write about Kurt in her autobiography), and eventually Vreeland hired Kurt to organize and catalogue her personal library. This job led to similar work for Mrs. Brooke Astor, the grand dame of New York society, as well as a story in *The New York Times* describing Astor's life and library.

Soon Kurt was working from home and cataloguing private libraries for book collectors great and frivolous—some with priceless collections of first editions, others with useless collections of *Reader's Digest* condensed versions. Whatever the value of these collections, Kurt became the man to see if you needed a library curated. He was now an emerging entrepreneur on a seemingly unstoppable upward trajectory.

Then the real world interfered.

Kurt's young son was diagnosed with autism and his wife with manic depression. Kurt's world spun out of control. His business slumped as he pumped his time and money into family affairs, and he had to file for personal bankruptcy. Before long, breaking under domestic pressures, he and his wife divorced and Kurt became a single father.

But difficult as it was to care for his son, there was a bright side. Kurt found that reading to his son hour after hour was therapeutic for father and son alike. As his son improved, so did his father's mood and hence life in general. Eventually, Kurt remarried a clothing designer and put his entrepreneurial skills to use by working with her to build her business.

Then at age of fifty-three, Kurt was bitten by a new entrepreneurial bug. Putting on his bookman's hat again, he realized that there was an unserved need for a bookstore in New York's traditional African-American neighborhood that specialized in books by and about African-Americans.

To start just such a bookstore, Kurt purchased a brownstone in Harlem. This proved to be a wise investment, as it allows Kurt to live above his place of work. His store has yet to turn a profit, Kurt tells us, but he has high hopes that he'll be profitable within the year.

All in all, when you look at Kurt's entrepreneurial career to date, you see someone who has had traditional employment, then evolved to home-based businesses with a commute down a flight of stairs. Overwhelmingly, Kurt feels that, given his personal situation and the needs of his family, having the freedom to work from home is, in his words, "manna from heaven."

Benefits of a home office

What are the actual benefits that make home-based offices so attractive to so many fifty-plus entrepreneurs?

Here's a list of favorites, culled from conversations we've had with retirement-age workers in a variety of fields. You may wish to add a few of your own entries to the list:

- Working in a home office gives you more control over the hours in your day and over the months on your calendar year.
- Operating a home office allows you to exchange the clamor of outside office life for a more private, low-key, easy-to-get-to and easy-to-be-in place of work.
- If you wish to spend more quality time with your children and/or grandchildren, and at the same time remain gainfully employed, a home office keeps the home fires burning.
- Running your own home operation means that you can choose which jobs you take on and which ones you don't, which items you sell, which items you manufacture, which

services you provide, and so forth. You set your own agenda. Your work stays new and interesting.
- If you want to remain at your longtime job on a reduced-time basis and simply supplement your current income, a home office allows you the best of both worlds.
- The savings both financial and to the planet in commuting-based gas consumption and pollution is an added perk.

There can be little doubt that the home office shoe fits a variety of feet and that, for many people turning the bend of retirement, it offers an ideal solution.

Of course, the question can also be asked: What if you are *not* in this category? What if you are an aspiring fifty-plus entrepreneur who prefers to leave your house or apartment every day and amble off to work in an office or factory or store or farm or on a subway or driving a car or riding in a truck? Then this chapter is not really for you.

Or perhaps it is, or at least it could be. At least give it a look. For no matter what work site you ultimately choose, it is always a good idea to keep your options open. You never know what your occupational future will bring. And remember, 5.6 million men and women over fifty years old today are self-employed. This figure represents a *twenty-three percent jump* since 1990. Approximately a quarter to a third of these independent contractors work at home. That's a lot of people when you think about it. Maybe they know something the rest of us don't.

So let's find out. First, we'll address some home office-related caveats. These vetted, we'll get to the fun part and look at the perks. Finally, we'll review some valuable advice on home office culture from people who know.

Five important things to think about before you open a home office

1. Be clear on what you mean by a home office.
The term "home office" is more or less generic. It can refer to a quilting shop in your attic or to a cabinet-making business you run from your garage. It can be a messenger service that you dispatch from

your apartment. It can be a back room in your house or apartment where you design dress patterns. It can be a small manufacturing plant on your home property. It can be outdoor work or indoor work. You can sit at a desk, stand at a counter, or work in the back room or over the phone. You can have a large number of face-to-face interactions with customers—or none at all.

Having a home business does not necessarily mean that you actually work from home or even that you have an office in your home, at least not exclusively. Think about Kurt Thometz, the bookseller. He now has his bookstore located downstairs in his house. At previous times, he worked mostly outside the home for wealthy book collectors but still, strictly speaking, had a home-based business. At still other times, he had jobs out of the house in bookstores but still did freelance work from home. The lines between home and office are not always that clear, and they can change constantly.

You may, for instance, start a fifty-plus career that's located at home, then, after several months jacking the business off the ground, spend most of your time visiting clients, making service calls, buying materials, whatever. This is an important point to note, especially if working exclusively at home is a priority.

Anne Homes's daughter and two granddaughters lived together for several years in Anne's four bedroom colonial house. Despite sharing a living space, Anne often felt that her busy schedule kept her from spending quality time at home. Having worked as a pastry chef for many years, Anne hit on an obvious solution: open a catering business in her own house. This way, Anne figured, she could put her work skills to good use and still have time left over to visit with her loved ones.

Using a combination of her own savings and borrowed funds, Anne installed food-preparation equipment in her garage, renovated her kitchen, acquired the needed licenses and permits, took on several part-time helpers, hired a chef, advertised, and opened her doors for business.

After a year, she was doing a brisk trade. The trouble was though, that from the very beginning she was forced to delegate food preparation duties to the chef, and to spend most of her time away from the kitchen—and hence the house—shopping, visiting potential customers, picking up pieces of equipment like coat racks and rented tables, and most time-consuming of all, attending her catered affairs. It did not take long for Anne to realize that having a home business did not automatically mean working at home.

There are, therefore, degrees of home "officing," just as there are degrees in everything that pertains to entrepreneurship. Being clear on this matter can be liberating.

2. Be sure to match the right home space to the right home business.

In their eagerness to open a home office, many fifty-plus entrepreneurs become overly enthusiastic, and hence unrealistic, about pursuing their dream job. They overlook the fact that it is extremely difficult to fit a business machine repair center into a bedroom, a locksmith service into a city apartment, a gymnastic center in a basement. It can be done, perhaps, but not very well.

Here are some tips for matching the right business to the right space and for compensating when the right amount of space is simply not available:

- It can save you time and money to realize from the start that certain businesses lend themselves to home-based work and certain kinds do not. There are no absolutes here, but there is common sense. In general, if your new planned business requires large amounts of inventory, has a massive customer inflow and outflow, uses massively large pieces of machinery, makes a great deal of noise, generates offensive odors, or handles quantities of toxic or chemical products, it's best to think about an away-from-home location.
- If you know what type of home business you'll be operating, do a walk-through of that section of the home or garage where your office, store, or shop will go. Plan out in advance where the necessary items will be arranged. Items that definitely require space include office furniture, business machines, storage bins, conference rooms, bathrooms, supply centers, vehicle stands, tool sheds, work equipment—it all depends on the type of business you're starting. The important thing is to plan it out in advance and in as much organized detail as possible. This

way, there will not be any unpleasant surprises when you start carting in the furniture and setting up the shelves.
- If you plan to receive sizeable amounts of mail, be sure that your mailbox is large enough to handle the flow. You may want to make use of a professional mailbox service or order an extra (or much larger) mailbox installed in your home to catch the overflow.
- Does your new business require that you keep a large stock of inventory at home? Do you have the space to store it all? If not you may find it convenient to rent storage space in a warehouse or less formally, in a neighbor's garage or storage shed. Just be sure you have enough room to keep your products organized and readily available.
- If you intend to rent storage space, especially self-storage space, there are several bottom-line features to look for in a facility. Location is crucial. You won't want to drive twenty miles, or take three busses, every time you pick up a few stored items. Make sure the storage area in question is well-lighted, open seven days a week, and protected by good security equipment. Does the facility offer month-to-month leases? (Beware of long-term contracts that may be difficult to break should a problem occur.) Does the facility offer pickup, delivery, and packing materials? Does the facility maintain a sprinkler system in case of fire? If your stored inventory is perishable, is climate control available? Is there on-site management—or at least a human being around—to speak with if you have a problem? You won't need all of these features, but you probably will need some.
- Do you plan to hold meetings and business conferences? Does your home base offer large enough accommodations to seat X number of clients or staff? If not, inquire about conference room rates at local hotels, conference centers, libraries, or even community centers at local parks and keep this information on hand. Talk to the people who staff these centers concerning costs, room availability, and the amount of advance reservation time required. Be sure to tour the facility to make sure it suits your needs.

Profile—Louise Pacheco is a wonderful cook who, while raising three children, often contributed dishes to functions at her church. People who tried her food loved it and began asking Louise to cater their private events like birthday and anniversary parties. Louise is not sure she wants to be a full-time caterer and take on the overhead of a professional kitchen. So she keeps her jobs small, and borrows kitchens from her neighbors for jobs she can't manage entirely in her own kitchen. She now has a home-based business that she enjoys, that makes a good profit, and that requires a minimal financial outlay to cover the fixed costs of rent and permanent staff.

3. **Be sure you have—and/or can get—all the licenses and permissions necessary for starting your business before you invest any money.**

Darrel Skates, a sixty-two-year-old retiree, wanted to turn a long-time hobby into a business by breeding wire-haired terriers in his house. Located on a busy residential street, he set up a kennel in his backyard and then, without checking to make sure the Board of Health and the town Zoning Board had any objections, went into the breeding business.

Two weeks later, three complaints from Darrel's neighbors were sitting on the desk at the local Police Department. Two were for noise level—the barking was driving people crazy—and one for pervasive animal waste smell.

Not having applied for the requisite permits, Darrel was swiftly closed down and was forced to abandon his dream before he even had time to dream it.

Moral: Attend to all the prerequisite licensing, permits, regulatory compliance issues, and town or city zoning issues *before* you start. Also, if your new business is service-based, be certain that the products you use on the job are acceptable to municipal authorities. A self-employed plumber new to his area, for instance, received a rude shock when he plumbed a house with PVC pipe and was then told by a building inspector that PVC piping was prohibited in local residential homes.

Don't let this one slide.

4. Avoid letting your choice of home business be influenced by other people's personal agendas.

When preparing to start your own home business, you may hear a variety of critical opinions disguised as friendly advice. This advice can come from friends, family, business associates, or turnkey home businesses anxious to see your name on their contract. The following messages should all raise a red flag:

> **Message:** A home business after fifty should *challenge* you. Don't take the easy route—find work that pushes you to new heights of career achievement.
>
> **Seeing through the message:** As to the challenges, you've faced plenty of these in your work life already. Do you need more? That's entirely up to you. Your new career should push your limits *only if* you want it to push your limits. If you prefer to run a home business that's slow-paced, part-time, and allows you idle hours to pursue your hobbies, family life, and peace of mind, go for it.
>
> **Message:** A home business after fifty should free you from the *mechanical work habits* you formed through the years at your previous job. It should shake you up. It should help you reinvent the way you approach your work life and the world at large.
>
> **Seeing through the message:** Maybe your work habits are fine as they are. Not everybody wants to shake things up. There's a great deal to be said in life for the status quo.
>
> **Message:** A home business after fifty should bring out *your real money-making potential*. All these years that potential has been slumbering. Time to wake it up.
>
> **Seeing through the message:** Not everybody in the over fifty crowd wants—or needs—to make lots of money. Many people in this age group have worked for years and are now financially set. Others are almost set, but need a little extra. Still others want to work at home to stay active or to contribute to the community or to pursue a passion. Money does not *always* make the world go 'round.

Message: A home business after fifty should keep you *physically active* as well as mentally sharp. Don't become a couch potato in front of the computer or phone all day in your walled-off home office.

Seeing through the message: Exercise is good. We all know that, especially if you sit a lot. But nothing demands that physical exertion be a central part of your job description. It is all a matter of personal inclination.

Message: A home business after fifty should be *creative*. Don't settle for the work-a-day, paper-pushing routines you performed at the company for thirty years. Now is the time to find your inner creative voice and give it due expression.

Seeing through the message: If you're a creative person by nature, then work at a job that's creative. That's who you are. But if not, don't. Remember, just because your new business is home-based does not mean you have to think like Leonardo da Vinci. If people insist that a home business should make you more imaginative, more inspired, that you should take this opportunity to express your long-suppressed artistic side, and so forth, more often than not this is the person's own creative fantasies—and/or frustrations—speaking. Just do what makes you happy.

Message: A home business after fifty should support and nourish your *community*. Don't be selfish; find a new career at your age that helps other people.

Seeing through the message: There will always be people who enjoy sermonizing about how others should help the world. In matters of work, such people insist that since you are now a certain age, and since you have amassed a certain amount of money, and since life has been good to you, and since you have your health (while others don't), yada, yada, yada, it is now your *duty* to be of service. Again, if you tend toward public spiritedness and if you have a natural urge to help the world, a service-oriented home business is a natural choice. But don't let others pressure you in this direction. Most of all, be careful of people who try to shame you or make you feel guilty that your at-home enterprise is not "giving back to society." All too often, such people use these phrases as weapons to make others feel bad, and to make themselves look, oh, so virtuous.

5. Avoid those tempting home-business cons.

Rule number one: If a work-at-home offer sounds too good to be true, it is too good to be true. Actually, it's probably a come-on. It may even be a scam.

You've seen the ads and the headlines:

"Earn $1,000 a day working at home in your spare time for no money down."

"Hottest new home business opportunity! Turnkey packages. Minimal startup costs. No previous experience necessary. We supply everything you need."

"Take an hour a day three to four days a week and RETURN phone calls (from home) to people waiting for information from you. You'll talk to ten to twenty people per day and generate $1,500 to $3,500 per week or even per day."

Sound familiar? We find such solicitations peppered throughout entrepreneurial magazines front cover to back. We see them posted on local bulletin boards, in supermarkets, in Laundromats, even on telephone poles. We've all noticed them. How can you *not* notice them? And to tell the truth, many of us have read them and asked ourselves: Can this be true? Can I *really* make $3,000 a week? Working at home? What's the deal here anyway?

And that, of course, is precisely what these dream weavers want you to think. Their intent is to stop you in your tracks, grab your attention, and inject a tiny drop of curiosity into your brain. It's the old salesman principle: Get a foot in the door and you're halfway toward closing the sale.

The people who compose these ads are experts at exploiting the irrational sides of human nature. The more tempting the ads sound, the more outlandish and improbable, the more they set us wondering, saying to ourselves, "Hey, you never know."

Especially common is the rags-to-riches pitch. Such ads tend to be long, detailed, and personal, often taking up an entire page in a newspaper or magazine. The formula is always the same, with plenty of italics, bolds, and exclamation marks to bang home each startling claim. This formula, with endless possible variations, goes something like this:

Pitch One: Establishing rapport—"I was desperate, just like you. Not so long ago I was **broke**. In a last-ditch effort to stay afloat **I sold everything** I owned (including the gold watch my father gave me before he died, and my daughter's bedroom set, etc.). Using an idea I'd been working on for ten years, I opened my own (online, mail order, retail, service, consulting, phone order, etc.) business."

Pitch Two: Quick success—"**Within a year,** I was making $2,000 a day working at home. That's right, **$2,000 a day! From home! Sometimes more!** Soon, I was driving a Porsche, living with my family in a fifteen-room dream house, vacationing in the Bahamas, and **living out my dream**. After a couple of years, I had EVERYTHING I'd ever wanted in life."

Pitch Three: Secret formula—"How did I do it? It's simple. The product (business, service, kit, training program, software, selling scheme, secret ingredient, etc.) I offered to the public was **irresistible.** That's right, *irresistible!* It sold like hotcakes! I couldn't keep enough of it in stock to satisfy my customers!"

Pitch Four: Sharing my secret—"After a few years of gangbuster profits, after I'd fulfilled all my own personal dreams, I thought to myself, 'Hey, **why not give back what I was lucky enough to get**? Why not tell other people about this **fantastic money-making product** (business, service, kit, training program, software, secret ingredient) of mine, so that they can enjoy the kind of life *they've* always wanted?'"

Pitch Five: Big Promises—"You can start making as much money as I did **in just a couple of months**—maybe even weeks! But hey, I won't kid you. You'll have to work at it. Nothing comes free in life. But even just **five or ten hours a week** spent selling my product (scheme, business, kit, service, etc.) can bring in **many thousands of dollars a month**. Plus you'll have financial security and set your own work schedule. All in the quiet of your own home." Etc., etc.

Pitch Six: Proof and testimonials—"So what's the catch? There is no catch. Just look at the testimonials (statistics, newspaper articles, letters, reports, etc.) on the bottom of this page. And I have plenty more where these came from. People just like you, who needed a little help to find their way to fame and fortune." Yada, yada, yada.

Pitch Seven: Buy it now—"For just a minimum setup charge (down payment, training cost, service fee, kit price, materials charge, one-time only expenditure, etc.) that barely covers my own shipping and production costs, I'll send you **everything you need to be up and running at home right away** and making **cartons of money** with this remarkable new product!"

Pitch Eight: Send for it now before it's too late—"Don't delay. This exclusive offer is for a limited time only, one time only, supplies are limited, etc. And if you order now, I guarantee that within one week..." Blah, blah, blah.

That's more or less the pitch. No doubt you've read such an ad a number of times. It contains a majority of the seductions one is likely to come upon in work-at-home ad scams, including:
- **An appeal to a common bond**—"Hey, I was like you once. Broke, with nowhere to turn."
- **An appeal to the reader's financial worries**—"We all *need* more money."
- **An appeal to the reader's financial greed**—"We all *want* more money."
- **An appeal to the reader's fantasies**—"You can drive a Porsche, own a mansion, go on dream vacations." Etc.

- **An appeal to the reader's desire for an ideal work situation**—"Work when you want, be your own boss, set your own hours, spend the day in the comfort of your own home, vacation when you like." Etc.
- **An appeal to the reader's need for proof**—"Let me show you these testimonials, fact lists, statistics, examples, and newspaper articles." Most of them phony or outrageously exaggerated.
- **An appeal to the reader's lack of expertise or knowledge**—"No experience necessary, so easy a child can do it, I'll give you all the training you need."
- **An appeal to the reader's leisure dreams**—"Work only a few hours a week."
- **An appeal to the reader's desire for instant results and easy money**—"Become an overnight millionaire, no startup fees or money down, make thousands of dollars by doing practically nothing, go from zero to $223,149 in just twelve months." Etc., etc., etc.

Touches all the psychological bases, doesn't it?

And the result?

A certain number of readers hear these promises and think that maybe, just maybe, this one is for real (who knows?). Assuming they have nothing to lose, they send off for more information and in the process make mistake number one: providing their address, phone number, and email address, thus guaranteeing that their name will soon be flying around the country on one or more mailing lists, many of them to be sold to other work-at-home scammers.

Every year, the U.S. Post Office tells us, $427 billion dollars are bilked from the unwary by con artists selling home business rip-offs. That's a lot of money, and a lot of people. A recent bulletin from the people at AARP who spend a gratifyingly large amount of time rooting out scams aimed at people over fifty, describe the mechanics of four popular work-at-home swindles:

- **Medical billing centers**—You send money for software to run a bill collection service from your home. The scam artists promise that the market is "wide open" and they have "lined up" clients for you. In reality, you stand to lose your entire $2,000 to $8,000 investment. The software is only an assortment of forms and collection letters that anyone could design. The names of companies they send you are not clients; they take these names and addresses from the phone book.

- **Envelope stuffing**—This is the most common work-at-home scam, says the U.S. Postal Inspection Service. You send money and the "business" sends you information about earning money by stuffing envelopes at home. What you actually get are instructions to sell this scheme to others by placing ads in newspapers to illegally entice new victims. You make nothing unless you recruit others to work for you. Called multilevel marketing, this scam is much like an illegal Ponzi pyramid scheme.
- **Assembly or craft work**—You send money for supplies to assemble into products such as aprons, baby clothes, jewelry, or Christmas decorations. Sometimes you must buy the equipment from the promoter. You're told that there is a ready market for the products, or that the company will buy the products from you directly. The catch? Your items never meet "quality standards," or you must sell the items yourself.
- **Business opportunities**—You send money for information about starting a business from your home. The details are vague but the promises are big, including claims that "we will provide all the training you need." The catch? The fraudulent salespersons will constantly try to sell you more information about special "training and support systems" and "your personal coach." And think about it: Anyone who ever hatched a business idea that actually lived up to the grandiose claims made would never offer this information to thousands of strangers in the first place.

The AARP bulletin (see *http://aarp.org/money/careers/selfemployment/a2002-10-02-FraudsWorkatHome.htm*) finally concludes with the most chilling warning of all. "And sometimes," it tells us, "those who send money for any of these schemes receive absolutely nothing. They just get their money taken."

Forewarned is forearmed.

Eleven pieces of helpful advice for starting a home business after fifty

Now that we've addressed the most common challenges that fifty-plus entrepreneurs face when setting up a home career, let's reiterate a basic point: Working at home is a terrific idea for many people, an ideal way to solve the financial and career problems that crop up at retirement time. As with any major life undertaking though, it's sensible to go into this venture with eyes wide open; which means you will want to start your new career armed with all the technical, business, and social knowledge needed to achieve success.

The following section, based on interviews with dozens of fifty-plussers who started their own home-based business, is a distillation of the most important information exchanged during these sessions. Certain formulas, advice, procedures, and dos and don'ts come up in these discussions. Here are some of the most interesting and relevant:

1. Do your research.

Unless you are a total expert in every aspect of your new home business, spend a few months boning up on the financial, legal, commercial, technical, operational, and social sides of your new business. If possible, avoid a seat-of-the-pants approach.

We spoke with Arthur, a man in his late fifty's, just months after his home real estate appraisal business went belly-up. We talked about the mistakes he'd made, most of which, it turned out, were organizational.

Then I asked him a personal question: "What do you think was the biggest mistake you made?" Without hesitation, he replied, "Not knowing my business well enough when I started."

I asked him to explain.

"Real estate appraisal is a knowledge-heavy game," he said. "You have to know a lot of things about a lot of things—architecture, banking, reading blueprints, building materials. I'd been in the textile business for years. I thought the business knowledge I'd acquired there would get me through, that I'd sort of pick up the other information as I went along.

"I took the courses I needed to get my license, of course, but I wasn't all that well prepared when I opened my business. I didn't read up as I should have on changes in the industry. I didn't read the magazines and journals. I didn't pay enough attention to how mortgage rates were responding. I wasn't very familiar with things like surveys, local tax law, recognizing flaws and improvements in a building's construction. I just wasn't prepared."

Do your homework.

2. Don't hold back on getting professional help when you need it.

If you need legal help setting up your home business, hire a lawyer. Don't try to do it yourself. The same with organizing an accounting system, figuring out your company's tax structure, writing up a business plan, or mapping out an advertising strategy. The trick is knowing when you can go it alone, and knowing when you need assistance. Fortunately, the rule of thumb here is simple: If you think you need help, you do.

Don't be penny wise and pound foolish. The dollars you spend to construct a solid legal, financial, and organizational structure is money well directed, especially in a home business where the buck literally always stops with you.

3. Be clear on your startup costs before you start up.

Factor it all in, however small or large the costs for space, equipment, supplies, services, etc. may be: Computers, thumbtacks, cement mixers, business cards, salaries, mailing lists, printer cartridges, display cases, snow-removal services, jackhammers, a kiln, client entertainment, rents, cleaning services, consultant fees, buttons, batteries, floor wax, accounting, advertising costs, pens, gas, software, carpeting, postage, grass seed, knife sharpeners, on and on. Every item counts.

Now go over the list line by line to see what items you've forgotten to add.

Then have a knowledgeable friend or business consultant go over it with you.

No unpleasant surprises later on, please.

4. Consider writing up a business plan.

Even if you intend to run a modest operation at home, writing a business plan at the beginning can seriously help guide your ship. A business plan is a document that shows potential backers, lenders, and clients how your business will work, and why it's a good idea. A business plan lists investments, loans, and expenses; analyzes potential markets; lays out a business strategy; evaluates the competition; develops a marketing campaign (if necessary); organizes the company structure; and develops financial projections showing how much you need to invest, how much you will earn, and when you can expect to see profits.

In general, a basic business plan for a small home business has four parts:

- **A profile of the planned business**—How your business operates, what it sells, and/or what services it supplies; also, what needs it fills for consumers, how it beats the competition, its legal structure, its organization, its staff positions, and so forth.
- **Financial breakdown**—Startup costs, expenditures, monthly cash flow, salaries, rent and leasing costs, possible funding sources, and all things money-related.
- **Management**—Equipment you'll use, location of business, staffing, management strategy, scheduling, etc.
- **Marketing strategy**—What are your target buying audiences? What are your price points? What do you plan to do online? How will you use the media? What methods will you use to sell your product, to advertise it, promote it, to get known around town?

Though the prospect of writing a business plan may be intimidating for the uninitiated, the truth is it is relatively easy to put together on a basic level, and extremely useful, especially if you plan to raise capital or seek investors.

There are many do-it-yourself books out today on writing business plans including—please forgive the self-promotion—two written by co-author Edward Rogoff titled *Bankable Business Plans* and *Bankable Business Plans for Entrepreneurial Ventures*. Start here and then branch out.

You can also get help from the U.S. Small Business Administration online (*www.sba.gov*), as well as an organization known as SCORE that provides free online and face-to-face business counseling, mentoring, and training. Look at SCORE's website at (*www.score.org/index.html*) for directions to your nearest SCORE office.

5. Consider advertising.

Don't be shy about getting your name out. If your at-home business lends itself to promotion, get those leaflets and fliers flying. Take out an ad in the local daily, in a trade magazine, over the radio, wherever your target audience is looking and listening. Print up brochures, and pass out handouts. Put up signs at the local food market and instant photo shop. Arrange to be interviewed by the city newspaper. Give talks and demonstrations. Write articles. Join a civic group. Tell friends and associates what you're doing. Create a website. Generate a buzz. Let people know you're out there, and that you're good. It will make a difference.

6. Find out if your service or product is marketable before you invest your money.

Talk to potential customers before you make too many business commitments. As the slick-talking hero of the play *The Music Man* insisted, "You gotta know the territory!"

A Nepalese friend of ours, Ram Bahadur, a man in his early sixties, tells an amusing story that occasionally ends up being retold by us as a cautionary tale in classes at the Lawrence N. Field Center on Entrepreneurship. While working for many years as an agricultural engineer in the Indian province of Bihar, Ram noticed that whenever he traveled to certain rural parts of the state, there were no chickens or eggs for sale in the marketplace. Here was a business waiting for a taker, Ram thought when he saw this state of affairs. Provide eggs and chickens to undersupplied sectors of the state. Without any competition, profits will pour in.

As his retirement drew near Ram began to lay plans to leave his job and to start a poultry farm in Bihar. His plan was to raise chickens, package the chicken products, and sell them in rural stores around the state. Before he made a total commitment, however, he decided to do some in-the-field research with perspective buyers.

Sound policy. Perhaps a little too sound in this case. For after just a few days of traveling from town to town in rural Bihar state, and talking to the people there it became painfully apparent to Ram that his plan was a disaster waiting to happen. Why? Because many of the people living in these rural areas belonged to a Hindu caste that considered poultry taboo. Even keeping a chicken or two for eggs was forbidden.

There was a reason, my friend finally realized, why chickens were in such short supply in the markets of Bihar. It was a sin to eat them.

Moral? Talk to people first before you try to sell to them. Find out who your potential buyers are. Find out if they really *want* the services or products you intend to supply. Then if they do, ask them how you can do the job for them faster, better, and more cost-effectively than the competition.

Go into the field. Garner representative opinions. Hand out free samples to make people familiar with what you're selling. Show pictures of your product, give demonstrations, pass out leaflets, talk it up, and then see how people react.

The feedback you receive during these sessions will be equivalent to what you'd hear if you were running your own focus groups. And don't forget that private get-togethers, town meetings, local organizations, community events, online social networks, chat groups, and blogs are all excellent places to gather public opinion.

In short, test your market first, explain to others what you're doing, and gauge their receptivity levels. Let people give you their bright ideas, take stock, and then proceed—or retreat—accordingly.

7. Know your insurance options.

First-time home business operators often make the mistake of thinking their office is covered by home liability insurance.

It's not.

If a client visits your home office or workshop, then trips, falls, and is hospitalized, your insurance company is under no obligation to pay the bill. In fact, in some states the insurer can cancel your policy if it learns you are conducting business at home without reporting this fact to them.

Therefore, before you open the doors of your business, consider talking to an insurance expert about purchasing a business owner's policy or a home office policy to cover your flanks.

Note, too, that your theft and property home insurance do not cover items in a home office. This includes valuable items such as computers, machinery, money and securities, furniture, inventory, leased equipment, and the like. Again, talk to a qualified insurance person concerning coverage.

8. Consider working part-time.

There is nothing in the rulebook that says you *must* work full-time if you work at home. Indeed, if you are approaching retirement age and think it would be a groove to start a home business, there is no reason why you must automatically quit your regular job or work full-time at home.

Many fifty-plus entrepreneurial types have the best of both worlds, the first world being their current full-time job, the second being an at-home job pursued part-time, on the weekends, say, or in the evenings when the children and grandchildren have gone home or to bed.

Consider, for example, speaking to your boss about cutting down your in-office work hours and filling the gap by working X number of hours at home. Think, too, about negotiating with your company for a different work schedule, one that allows you to spend several hours each day working at home. Still another possibility is to purchase a franchise and hire someone to run it for you while you remain at your full-time job.

The important thing is to keep your scheduling options open. As far as home entrepreneurship goes, nothing is written in stone.

9. Create a comfortable home office environment.

You're going to be here a lot of the time—all day perhaps, and every day. Why not make the surroundings in your office or workshop as agreeable as possible? Here are some tips:

- **Furniture**—Purchase the best office chair you can afford. A poorly designed chair (i.e., one that's too soft, too hard, poorly angled, or has bad mobility) can cause a list of woes including carpel tunnel syndrome and low-back pain. Check out the Herman Miller Aeron chairs. They're expensive but generally considered the most comfortable office chair on the market. For information on picking a good office chair, check out the following online site: *http://freshome.com/2007/05/11/computer-chair-buying-guide-a-step-by-step-guide/*). After your chair, a desk with a generous amount of working space plus adequate storage areas is essential. Also in the storage department, think about utilizing large plastic containers, bookshelves, a pegboard for hanging tools, and unused household closet space. (As a rule of thumb, if you use an object frequently, keep it within easy reaching distance. If not, store it out of sight. The less clutter, the clearer the mind.)

- **Air circulation**—Breathing is good. You'll want to do it in an unobstructed way with adequate ventilation. Pick a spot for your desk or working space that's not too stuffy or cramped. Make sure your workplace allows for maximum air circulation. Avoid basement work areas if possible. They tend to be stuffy and damp. If your office must be located in a tight, cramped space, consider using a floor or desk fan to keep the air circulating freely.
- **Room temperature**—Air conditioning (or fans, swamp coolers, etc.) in the summer and adequate heating in the winter are essential. You never want it too hot or too cold. Extreme temperatures numb the brain. They can also interfere with office equipment performance, especially printers and computers. Baseboard heat is less drying on the nasal membranes than forced hot air. If you get tired of the air conditioner's muffled hum in the summer, consider turning it off for a while and opening your screened windows to the world.
- **Light**—Natural light is best. It saves on the electric bill, provides full-spectrum light, and builds cheer. If your office has windows, position your desk nearby. You may need no other light sources, at least during the day. If you do intend to use artificial light, tungsten bulbs are best. Just be sure the lighting provides enough illumination to keep your eyes happy. And one health-worthy suggestion: Avoid fluorescent lights. They're cheap to buy and run, yes, but

the light they produce is murder on the eyes, the whining buzz they generate is a nuisance to the ears, and, according to many laboratory tests, fluorescent flicker exerts a negative effect on office workers' moods. Radiation in the form of X-rays is also emitted from fluorescent tubes, causing a slow clustering of blood cells in the brain and a consequent reduction in oxygen flow, making people feel drowsy and depressed as the day goes by. Go the natural-light route whenever you can.

- **General environment**—Consider all of the following elements: Color on the walls, neatly organized records and papers, plenty of roomy file cabinets, neatly arranged books on the shelf, easy-to-read labels, pleasant pictures on the walls, plants and greenery at the windows, a clock that's visible from all points in the room, important items in your workspace positioned within easy reach, a minimum of cords and wires to trip over (think wireless), a really attractive and highly usable phone, an ergonomically friendly desk. Ask yourself: What can I do to make my workspace more effective, comfortable, and attractive? Then do it.

10. Take advantage of the IRS's home office tax deduction.

The IRS allows a deduction for "the business use of your home." But you must meet their requirements to qualify. Get to know these ground rules thoroughly, as things can get a little tricky in this area.

Here, in brief, is a list of things you should know about taking this neat deduction. When tax time comes, talk to your accountant concerning the details.

- You must show the IRS that 1) your home is your principal place of business, and 2) the workspace you are deducting is being used exclusively for business. Definitions can blur here, though, generally speaking, if you work in your home office three days a week or more, the IRS will accept your claim.
- If you use your home or a structure on your home site for storing equipment and/or inventory, you can deduct this space *even* if you do not use it exclusively for business.

- If your house is not your principal place of business, but if you use it regularly to meet with customers, clients, sales reps, patients, etc. you may still qualify for the home office deduction.
- The amount you can claim on the home office deduction depends on the amount of space you use for business within your home. For instance, if your home work space is twenty feet by twenty feet in a house that is 2,000 square feet large, divide the square footage of the work space (twenty times twenty in this case, giving you 200 square feet) by 2,000 (the size of the house), and you get ten percent, which equals a ten percent tax deduction.
- In case of a tax audit, be prepared to prove the legitimacy of your deduction. Keep business records on hand, make sure all business mail is sent to your home address, take pictures of your working space, maintain a log of business clients who visit you, and order a separate phone line and email address for your home business.
- A book that will help you understand the home business exemption in depth is Stephen Fishman's *Home Business Tax Deductions: Keep What You Earn*.

Here's a short list of items you can deduct if you run a home business. There are plenty more, but this will get you started:
- Business insurance
- Bank charges for business accounts
- Interest on all business debts
- Business vehicles
- Business-related education: courses, online tutorials, and seminars attended
- Gas and mileage spent on business
- Social Security payments
- Business-related subscriptions, books, and journals
- Charitable contributions made in the name of your business
- Taxes such as sales tax on business purchases, excise taxes, real estate taxes, and more

- Business operation costs: telephone and online services; postage and/or shipping costs; rented or leased equipment or services; advertising and PR; repairs to your home office or its equipment as well as equipment depreciation; travel expenses including tolls, licenses, and permits; Blackberries; computer-related materials such as disks, flash drives, software, etc.; and moving costs.

Last tips

We've covered a lot of the essential business bases so far in this chapter. As with any complex and layered subject, however, there is always more to know about starting a home office. The following hints and advice, most of it gathered from interviews conducted with successful fifty-plus home entrepreneurs, will tie up loose strings and add more information to your growing knowledge bank.

- **Keep your work life and home life separate**—One of the major challenges that home office entrepreneurs report is keeping the home office environment and the home itself separate. We're talking here about a child or grandchild playing games on your computer or rummaging through those important piles of receipts; about friends who know you're at home now and who just happen to drop a bit too frequently; about the temptation to get up every ten minutes, rifle through the fridge for snacks, watch a favorite soap opera, chat with your spouse, or read a magazine. You get the point. The only way to confront this blurring of borders is to draw up rules and routines for yourself and family members and then stick to them. Discipline, discipline, discipline. For example, let other people in the household know that you are not to be disturbed from hour X to hour Y. Keep the door of your shop or studio or office closed during work hours, and if necessary, locked. Allow yourself a limited number of eating breaks, and put a governor on the time you spend visiting with others in the house each day. Also, keep household paperwork such as home bills, letters, insurance forms, magazines, private mail, catalogues, etc. out of your office. In fact, keep *everything* relating to your home separate from your office environment. Use common sense here, and stick to your own rules.

- **Avoid overwork**—While some fifty-plus entrepreneurs spend too much of their home work time dallying or giving into temptations, others become workamaniacs, laboring twice as hard now as they did at their previous out-of-the-house job. Certainly it's difficult at first getting things to run the way you want them to, but it's also important to pace yourself. Take breaks during the day. Set limits on your work hours. Schedule mini-vacations. Reduce stress. Burnout never did anybody—or any business—any good.
- **Make full use of today's technology**—Technology is the home office entrepreneur's best friend. Like or not, to stay ahead in any modern business, electronics are a must: computers, printers, phones, answering machines, voice mail, scanners, faxes, the works. If you happen to be computer shy, as some members of the fifty-plus world can sometimes be, work to overcome it. Hire a techie to show you the cyber ropes. Take computer classes. Read computer magazines. The hard fact is that in today's competitive marketplace, most home businesses—not all, perhaps, but a vast majority—are hampering themselves severely, perhaps fatally, if they do not put the best of today's technology to work for them.
- **Take courses, give courses**—Now that you're out of the workplace and operating from home, you're probably not talking to as many people in your field as you once did. A good way to compensate is to keep learning—that is, to take classes, participate in study sessions, online training, seminars, and/or demonstration groups, whatever keeps your skills well honed. Also, as the proverb goes, "we learn by teaching." If you have a skill, share it with others at your local college, in extended-learning seminars, via magazine articles you've written. The more you interact with other people in a give-and-take way, the sharper your new and old work skills will become.

Chapter 6
Networking for Building a Solid New Business

Rule number one
Entrepreneurship, like it or not, want it or not, is a team sport. You cannot—and should not—do all the work. Thus the entrepreneur's number-one rule: Take advantage of the resources you already have.

Okay, sure, you could spend ten years in your laboratory basement perfecting cold fusion. You could trek across the Gobi until the inspiration for a recipe for a zero-calorie chocolate brownie reveals itself to you. But even in these cases, you will ultimately need help from other people to patent, market, and commercialize the fruits of your solitary genius. The people who help you at this task, whether with cold fusion or opening a bakery, are part of your team. Find them, and form your own personal network.

Now the great news!

You've already done most of the heavy lifting.

As a fifty-plus entrepreneur, you have worked for years and have already built your own personal network of contacts, colleagues, organizations, and business associates.

This cast of characters is now standing in the wings waiting to help you build your new venture and make it a success. With a bit of luck and some right-minded planning, this network will be a potent resource for you, a source of willing friends and sympathetic colleagues who provide advice, guidance, financial aid, connections to others, and personal support.

Let us introduce you to Maxine Martens.

Maxine started a new business when she was fifty-four years old. After only four months, she had eight employees on her staff, was turning a profit, and was running a tremendously successful company that allowed her to divide her time between New York and leading cities around the world.

But let's start at the beginning.

Maxine was born and raised in south Florida. When she graduated from the University of South Florida in the early 1970s with a business degree, she found her skills in great demand. After considering eight juicy business offers she decided to give retailing a try. Within two years of taking a job at a department store chain, she was promoted to swimwear buyer. "It's hard to fail as a swimwear buyer for a chain in Florida," she said with a laugh.

Maxine married a few years later and moved to London to support her husband in his career. The couple then ended up living in Cairo for two years and Paris for five. From these experiences, Maxine fell in love with large, cosmopolitan cities and international travel.

After returning to the United States seven or eight years later, Maxine resumed her business career in retail as a buyer for Marshall Field's, but the job did not work out. "It simply was a bad fit of culture and personality," she said.

Maxine then called the headhunter firm that placed her in the Marshall Field's job. The CEO of the company remembered her and how strong her people skills were. He hired her on the spot!

This new job turned out to be an exceptionally good fit. Maxine's work in retail, her extensive travel, and, most of all, the large personal network she had built over the years served as a strong base while searching for hirable executives in the fashion, retail, and beauty industries. Maxine worked as a headhunter for a dozen years and finally decided it was time to start her own business.

Before taking the first steps in this direction, however, she sat down and made a list of benefits she wanted from a job.

She needed to earn a good living, of course. That was number one. But she also wanted to travel regularly to the cities she loved and to visit the friends she had made there. She likewise wanted to work with people she enjoyed and with whom she felt a common bond of values. Finally, she wanted to run her own show. Enough of working for other people—now it was time to set her own course.

To make all this happen, Maxine's mother took an $80,000 home equity loan on her home and Maxine dug into her Rolodex. She put her substantial selling skills to work with existing clients and others in her network. In a year and a half, she had seventy-five clients.

Today Maxine's Rolodex has grown to occupy a large area of her hard-drive, and her Blackberry holds 1,800 contacts. Her office computer network tracks thousands of executives in target industries, along with every interaction she and her associates have with them. Most importantly, Maxine has turned the company she started, Martens & Heads!, into one of the top executive search firms in her sector.

What was the basic formula for Maxine's success?

She had industry knowledge, great people skills, an ability to close a sale, and a strong management aptitude—all important assets. Most importantly though, Maxine had built a multitude of personal connections with all the right people on both sides of the equation—with companies seeking to hire and with people seeking to be hired. This network was built during years of working as a headhunter in other people's firms. It was constructed by polishing her social skills, by making friends, by keeping records, and then by using the contacts she'd made to keep making more. It takes gold to make gold.

Taking your network inventory

You may not, of course, own a Blackberry with 1,800 names in it. But if you are an experienced fifty-plus career starter who has done a reasonable amount of meeting and connecting throughout your business life, you still have plenty of allies, some of whom you may not have even thought about. Let's take a quick inventory:

- **Business colleagues**—Naturally, many of the contacts you made in your business past would be impossible to find today. But many others are still in the places you left them—at the office, the firm, the bank, the store, the insurance company, the real estate agency, the supply depot, the delivery service, the executive offices, the client list. Lots of people. Hundreds, perhaps. So use them. They are your strongest networking resource.

- **Family**—Do you remember the last family wedding you attended? How many people were present to toast the bride and groom? A hundred? Three hundred? Think about it. These people are all part of your potential network because they are family or, indirectly, because they are friends of the family. This is not to mention the cousins and friends of cousins who were absent that day. Or remotely related relatives. Or people who live far away. Or family members you share holiday cards and occasional calls with but not much else. The time is now to reach out, even to the very edges of the family circle.
- **Friends**—Perhaps you keep a list of holiday names in your computer or in an old dog-eared card file with addresses and phone numbers of friends. We're not necessarily talking about close friends here, just people with whom you are currently acquainted or have known in the past. These are the people with whom you coached little league or people with whom you went to school. These may also be neighbors, former neighbors; former boyfriends and girlfriends (well, maybe); people with whom you play poker or pinochle; people who belong to your club; people with whom you go golfing or take classes or watch sports or shop or hike or sing or go to church or synagogue ... You get the picture. All these people are potential members of your network.

The next step

Now you put your network into hyper drive by using a popular web-based social networking site such as *Facebook* or *LinkedIn*.

If you are a member of one or more of these sites, you already know what a powerful, no-cost opportunity they afford to connect with numbers of people new and old, *and* to connect through your existing network with the networks of friends and colleagues. All you have to do to use this incredibly powerful resource is sign up, sign in, and then provide basic information such as your line of work, where you went to school, and most importantly, the people you already know. The latter task will activate automatically if you have an address book that the website can connect to. Then ... *whir* ... *whiz* ... and you are connected through the site to those names you have in your address book *and*—fantastic bonus—to the people *these* people know.

Every social networking site has a slightly different approach to bringing people together. *Facebook* and *MySpace* originally started with young people, and this site more or less still caters to this age group. *Plaxo* and *LinkedIn*, meanwhile, are oriented more to businesspeople and professionals. *Twitter* focuses on frequent, quick interaction among its members. Others—and there are many—focus on a region of the world, a specific country, a professional group, an industry, an ethnic population, or an age cohort. Many professional organizations have their own networking facilities.

There are many ways to use social networking sites. You can stay in touch with business contacts you know or have known in the past. You can ask people in your network to introduce you to key people they know. Or you can search for someone you wish to meet through another's network connections. The important thing is to get started, and to use this amazingly powerful (and free) resource to its limits.

Little networks built large networks

Take the case of John Lamie, a man now in his sixties who, at age fifty-seven, became the founder, president, and only full-time employee of a highly successful business venture known as Asia Dispensing.

While working for companies such as Elizabeth Arden and Paco Raban for many years, John enjoyed a successful career in the packaging business. If you have ever sprayed perfume into the air or pumped hand cream from a high-end cosmetic dispenser, you've probably used a device that he helped design and manufacture.

After a long career with several large packaging companies, John began to take an objective look at both his profession and his professional situation. He drew some hard conclusions.

First, the higher you go in a large organization, the higher the b.s. factor becomes.

Second, this dishonest atmosphere saps you of passion for the work you truly love.

Third, the way out of this dilemma is to start your own business.

Fourth, the risk of starting your own entrepreneurial venture is real, yes, but this danger is strongest during startup. Think things through, have a good business plan, and, over time, a carefully managed business will deliver the kind of financial and psychological rewards that are simply not available to people who work at large corporations.

In 2005, John Lamie took the leap.

A respected client had once told him he was a "solution-finding kind of guy." Taking this testimonial to heart, he started brainstorming new business ideas from backward to forward; that is, he tried to determine which particular solutions best fit which specific problems he had encountered in the packaging industry.

Eventually, John decided that the solution a majority of American packaging companies needed most was to find a successful way of doing business with China, which in 2005 had already become the world leader in package production.

Business standards and practices in China, John knew from experience, were often diametrically opposed to those in the West. What was considered fair and normal practice among Chinese companies was often perceived as unfair and unethical in the West—and vice versa. There were also the bugbears of culture clash, political suspicion, personal mistrust, and of course, language differences. While access to low-cost quality package manufacturing in China was attractive to American cosmetics companies, doing business there on a day-to-day basis clearly required a crash course in cultural social relations.

But then, John Lamie was a solutions guy.

As per his plan, John started out by contacting packaging factories in China and establishing personal phone relations. Then he traveled to various Chinese cities to meet the people in his industry and to inspect their facilities.

Once he made these contacts and secured friendly relationships with Chinese colleagues, John got in touch with his own business contacts at home, seeking their help, advice, and financial support. To reinforce this existing (and ever-growing) network of allies, customers, and associates, John also launched a newsletter that provided a highly informative overview of important trends and news in the American packaging industry. This project helped position him as an expert in the field, and made him visible to thousands of potential customers who might otherwise never have known his name.

Finally, John set up a website for his new company that offered useful information to readers and, just as importantly from a networking perspective, allowed people in his industry to learn about his company and to contact him quickly and directly.

John Lamie, in short, used his existing network connections to build an even bigger network, and then worked it to the max. Next year, John tells us, Asia Dispensing Company with its one employee expects to have over $50 million in revenues.

How did he do it? Networking, networking, networking.

Networking from scratch

Suppose you are entering an industry that is largely unfamiliar to you and in which you have few contacts, friends, or associates.

Say, for example, that you are a video producer who has worked in television news for many years. Because of a growing need, you decide that you want get into the business of selling your services to webmasters that use video on educational websites. While these two fields are related in certain ways, educational video and news video are basically different animals. This means that at the beginning you will probably not know a lot of people in the educational website business, and few if any of your friends or second cousins will be in the business either.

Where to begin? By making personal contacts.

For example, read the newsletters, websites, search sites, and trade journals related to your new field of interest. Find out when conferences and association meetings are being held that draw people involved in website education.

Then attend them. Browse around. Ask questions. Start conversations. Dialogue with reps and vendors and bystanders. Think social. Attend networking events: Lectures, demonstrations, presentations, and seminars. Go to business-associated cocktail parties and dinners. Talk to the person to the right of you there and the one to the left. Simply rubbing shoulders with a stranger in the elevator at a meeting or trade show can lead to casual conversation and then to, well, who knows?

What is the best way to exploit these meetings and to make the most of them?

First and foremost, tell the people you meet in a simple, short, and direct way what you do. Ask them what they do. Since everybody is attending these affairs for basically the same reasons, helpful conversations will follow as a matter of course as you exchange ideas, pick brains, and discuss ways in which you can be mutually helpful.

Of course, instant rapport does not happen with every person you meet. But it really does happen, and this is how the game is played. You may have to kiss a few frogs before you meet your princes and princesses, but remember, other people at these affairs are just as anxious to add you to their network as you are to add them. It's a mutual thing. Everybody profits from networking.

So let's review the process:
1. Figure out the type of people affiliated with your new business that you most need to meet.
2. Find out where these people congregate: their associations, meetings, conferences, clubs, and social get-togethers of one kind or another.
3. Make an effort to meet these people and to tell them what you do.
4. Encourage conversation concerning what they do, what you do, and how the two of you can help each other.

Targeted networking

Sometimes you will know exactly which people you need to meet in your new profession.

The key person here may be the president of a certain company, the vice president of a division that uses what you sell, an important rep, a consultant, a media person, even a client—whoever. The idea is to make direct one-on-one contact with this key person and present yourself to this person in an interesting, personable, and compelling way.

Face-to-face networking with key people, if done properly, can bring quick and gratifying success. This holds especially true if you are a middle-aged or older businessperson, as studies in the social sciences suggest that executives and people in authority tend to pay more attention to the requests of experienced people than those who are young and just starting out.

The targeted method requires that you approach your target knowing exactly how you need to appear physically, which selling points you *must* get across, and perhaps most importantly, what you can say to the person in question that will make you seem useful and helpful. There is an old bit of wisdom in the film business that maintains that if you're a screenwriter trying to sell your screenplay, you'd better be able to condense the entire script idea into a single paragraph. This is known in some circles as your "elevator speech," meaning your pitch has to be brief enough to convey during the time it takes to ride an elevator straight from the bottom to the top of an average building.

If your plot summary is too long, too wordy, or too complicated, you'll quickly lose your audience; the same applies to networking. Say what you need to say in a precise, informative, and succinct way—then step away from the proverbial podium.

Working cold contacts is, of course, a tough and scary proposition. It's tough because many important people are too busy, standoffish, difficult to reach, and sometimes just damned nasty. They don't answer their phones. They don't respond to emails or letters. Their assistants are overly protective. They shout at you and hang up on you.

Rejection, rejection, rejection.

There is a simple solution, however: Get over it! Take the risk. Just do it; then do it again and again and again. "If you don't like the heat," the saying goes, "jump into the fire." If you're rejected, well then, it's that person's loss. No reason to take it personally. There will be plenty of others who will see the importance of your business idea and its value. It's kissing frogs again. So pucker up. The right person will come along.

Finally, by means of summing up, here is a simple five-step process for turning cold contacts into names in your address book:
1. Identify the people you most need to reach.
2. Acquire all necessary contact information for them: address, email, phone number, etc. (You may not be able to get all this information, but you can certainly get some of it.)
3. Contact your key people with a short, simple, clear message about what you do and why you can be of service to them.

4. Ask the person's permission to schedule a call or meeting.
5. Follow up, follow up, and follow up some more. You must be persistent here; persistent to the point of feeling embarrassed. Some people will put you off because they are busy, some people want to test you to see if you're serious, and some are just rude. Just keep trying until you find those decent princes and princesses. They're out there somehow, somewhere—guaranteed.

Chapter 7
The Franchise

For the record

Not long ago, we were having a lively conversation with a colleague at Baruch College on the pros and cons of buying a franchise. In the middle of the discussion, this fellow came out with an odd non sequitur.

"A guy walks up to you in a bar," he declared, "and says he wants to make a bet. You ask him what he wants to bet on.

"The man informs you that he has an uncanny psychic talent. He can look at any old vinyl record, any record in the world—a vintage jazz record, say, or something by the Grateful Dead. In a second or two, he'll tell you exactly how many grooves the recording has on its surface. Five bucks says he can do it right now.

"Needless to say, this man is making an impossible claim. How, you think to yourself, can anyone instantly count the thousands of circles on a vinyl record? And thus, how could anyone lose such a wager betting against him? So you shake hands and the bet is on.

"Then the man, who just happens to have an old Kingston Trio record tucked away in his knapsack, whips it out, glances at it for a moment, and with great flourish, announces that 'My extraordinary visionary faculties tell me that this particular record has ... *one* groove!'

"Which, of course, is true. Like all records, it has a single spiraling groove that begins at the outer rim of the recording and ends at the center.

"The point I want to make here," our storyteller continued, "is that some franchises are like classic sucker bets: When you hear them described you think you can't possibly lose, when in reality you can't possibly win."

Point taken. Franchises can sometimes be a tricky and even deceptive deal.

The best of them, the ones that are well established, intelligently structured, skillfully managed, and sincerely dedicated to working in harmony with their chain franchises offer an excellent route to business ownership. They keep proprietors happy, earn them a good living, and sometimes make them rich.

The worst franchises, on the other hand, are indeed like sucker bets. During the recruitment stage, reps from these companies pull out all the stops to persuade you that their franchise is an absolute no-miss deal. Convinced, you sign up; at which point you discover that there was a lot of fine print you didn't read, and that, in fact, your contract is structured in such a way that no matter how hard you work the best you can hope for is to break even—or worse.

So, franchise buyer, beware.

At the same time, franchise buyer, do your homework, keep an open mind, get good professional advice, and in the end you may find yourself buying into a terrific second career.

In good company

If you do decide to purchase a franchise, you will not lack for company.

At the present time, there are approximately 1,500 companies in the United States that sell franchises and 750,000 chain businesses that operate them. This number is growing every year. Every eight minutes, a new franchise opens its doors in the United States. Franchises, what's more, keep almost 20 million people employed. They generate more than a trillion-and-a-half dollars each year. They produce forty percent of all service-related revenues. And they account for almost fifty percent of retail sales in the United States. One out of every twelve businesses in this country is a franchise. Of these, men and women over fifty run more than a third.

In the pages that follow, we will take a look at franchising from the standpoint of the fifty-plus entrepreneur. You will learn how franchises work and what type of expenditures and profits you can expect to make from them. You'll learn the procedural ins and outs you'll need to know at the beginning, and how you can make your accumulated business acumen work for you in the franchising world. We'll also review for you the pros and cons of franchising, with an eye toward helping you decide precisely how well suited it is to your skills, your experience, and your stage of life.

The ABCs of franchising

You may already know a good deal of what we're going to tell you in the next few pages about franchising. Or you may not. It depends on your past business experience. Either way, it never hurts to review important information on the subject of franchises and to be crystal clear on its basics.

A franchise is a marketing system that allows one party—known as the *franchisee*—to use the name, logo, product, advertising, reputation, and operating systems of another party—the *franchisor*.

This agreement is contractual, highly structured, and, in the best of all possible worlds, designed to financially benefit both parties. The average length of a contract between a franchisor and a franchisee is ten years.

The legal tie that binds this arrangement is set in place the moment a franchisor licenses its name and facilities to a franchisee. Besides sharing the power of the franchisor's brand and the outreach of its marketing systems, franchisees receive a variety of benefits and supports such as site construction, staff training, promotions, advertising, special events, and more. These benefits differ widely from company to company and are usually pegged to the buying price of the franchise. The more you pay, the more you get.

The franchisee, in turn, agrees to purchase the franchise at a given cost. The franchisee also agrees to abide by the franchisor's operational rules as spelled out in the contract, and to pay the franchisor a certain percent of its profits, usually from three to six percent of the monthly gross.

The average initial price of a franchise in the United States is around $250,000, though investments can be as low as $5,000 for, say, an upholstery-cleaning business or a monthly coupon magazine. They can also be as high as a million dollars plus for the big guys on the block, a Starbucks or a McDonalds (the latter is now the largest franchise company in the world). Note, however, that since the economic downturn started in 2008, prices have taken a corresponding dip in franchise buy-ins, and today, certain blue-chip franchises are a bit easier—and cheaper—to acquire.

Broadly speaking, the franchisee—the person who buys the franchise—can be an individual, a partnership, a family, even a consortium. In real life, franchisees are usually single individuals, often individuals at midlife or older who are looking for the security and ready-to-go marketing power of an established business.

These individuals may have prior experience doing what the franchise does, or they may not. The franchise may be a successful small business that is growing rapidly. It may be a mid-level company that runs, say, 400 stores in thirty states. Or it may be a mega-giant that maintains 100,000 stores worldwide.

When considering the ins and outs of a franchise purchase, it's important to note that the quality of franchisors in the United States runs a *very* wide spectrum.

The least substantial have little or no brand recognition. They are usually inexpensive to operate, providing a do-it-in-your-basement occupation such as wood refinishing or document lamination. They are also cheap to purchase, sometimes suspiciously cheap. Most of all, they offer easy acceptance to applicants. All that's required is the price of admission. Indeed, an easy acceptance policy is frequently advertised as a key hook in a low-cost franchise's pitch: everyone qualifies. There is little or no screening, no interviews, and no background checks.

Fine.

But then once you sign up, some franchisors tend to more or less forget you, and there is little or no follow-up. Perhaps they provide a day or two of training, a flimsy training manual, a homemade-style video, and a few phone conversations. That's it. Eventually, the new franchise owner discovers that his "partner" is more interested in selling franchises than in running them. Such companies, it becomes clear, are actually in the business of selling franchises. They'd like to see you stay afloat financially, obviously, so they can keep receiving their franchise fees. But as far as they're concerned, they've made their principal profit up front by selling you the franchise. The rest is gravy.

This is not to say that all inexpensive franchises are irresponsible. Many are very responsible. It *is* to say that, as a general rule, the cheaper the buy-in price of a franchise, the fewer benefits and less attention you are likely to receive after the sale is made.

Well-established, high-profile franchises, on the other hand, operate at the reverse end of the spectrum.

Entrepreneur Magazine's 2008 Picks for the ten most successful American franchises:

1. 7-Eleven, Inc.
2. Subway
3. Dunkin' Donuts
4. Pizza Hut, Inc.
5. McDonald's
6. Sonic Drive In Restaurants
7. KFC Corp.
8. InterContinental Hotels Group
9. Domino's Pizza, LLC
10. RE/MAX, Inc.

Where the low-end guys take your money and run, high-enders take your money and stay—and stay—and stay, monitoring your postpurchase operations in lock step every inch of the way. These companies have gone to great lengths to standardize their business M.O., developing high-recognition architecture, advertising, logos, graphics, equipment, uniforms, service agendas, seating arrangements, slogans, and so forth, all of which provide the public with the uniformity, consistency, and predictability it so craves. If perchance new franchise owners veer off into "creative" operational methods, or if they simply slack off, franchisors know from experience that shoddy performance in one outlet causes customer confidence in *all* outlets to plunge. They are thus correspondingly strict with their franchisees—downright Draconian in some cases.

Simply to qualify for a high-end franchise can be a grueling experience, especially if you are attempting to buy into a super giant like Wendy's or Subway.

The franchisor will, for instance, want to take a deep look into your financial records, your net worth, and your liquid capital assets. The company may want you to have industry experience related to the job (although sometimes it prefers that you have no experience, so you can be trained their way from the ground up). It will usually want you to display strong social and leadership skills plus have a solid grounding in general business practice. Interviews will be performed, probably several of them. Some franchisors administer psychiatric personality tests. Be prepared for a grilling.

Once you've run the gauntlet of the selection process and have received the corporate seal of approval, the company will keep steady tabs on every detail of your operation. They will choose the location of your new business. They will dictate building codes and specifications. They will perform frequent inspections, oversee employee selection, and provide rigorous staff training. They will set the prices you can charge and salaries you can pay. They will conduct continual rounds of meetings and reviews, supply mandatory advertising and promotions (usually at the franchisee's expense), and much more, all depending on the franchisor in question.

Tight, careful, constant, and sometimes intrusive monitoring is therefore the price you pay for the name and security that high-end franchises offer.

Seen in a positive light, this micromanagement can be a wonderful thing. It provides new players with a time-tested business model. It helps them make their way through the complexities of starting and running a new business. The big franchisor's national reputation reduces risk on the franchisee's investment. Finally, and most importantly, a brand-name franchisor can more or less assure its franchisee a healthy income flow. The largest companies in the country like Dunkin' Donuts and Kentucky Fried Chicken claim they have never sold a franchise that (if run according to their exact instructions) did not make money.

People in the fifty-plus category who are used to working for a large firm and who are comfortable taking directions from higher-up, often find themselves quite happy working for a large franchisor. These organizations offer security, dependability, a paint-by-number operational blueprint, and, in most cases, solid profits.

On the other hand, members of the fifty-plus generation who want to be their own boss may find big franchises stifling. People in this category are best advised to search for a company that offers a relatively large amount of operational freedom and creativity. As usual, the choice depends on one's goals, temperament, and needs.

Pros and cons of franchising 101

Continuing our somewhat inquisitorial analysis of franchising, we can ask the question in further detail: What are the major up sides and what are the major down sides of buying into a franchise?

This is a central issue and one that has special resonance for members of the fifty-plus generation. The following pros and cons, with corresponding variations, are common to most of the franchises you are likely to consider:

Pro One: You are buying an already established, profit-making business operation.

A printing service, a gas station, an automobile dealership, a UPS store, a Quiznos sandwich shop, a house cleaning service—it doesn't much matter. By definition, the franchise you are acquiring has an established track record, effective marketing methods, and at least some degree of name recognition.

Even if the franchise is small and little known, if your research shows it's been operating for a while, posts good sales figures, and maintains genial franchisor-franchisee relationships, you can be relatively sure their system works.

Good franchisors have honed their management and selling techniques down to a science. They have done all the hard work for you in advance.

Result? The franchisee *instantly inherits* selling tools that many businesses struggle for years to develop. These tools are proven to work; they sell product. Thus, the big three benefits—consistent profits over time, effective business strategies, and recognized brand name—are the main attractions you are paying for in your initial investment.

Pro Two: You are buying a turnkey operation.

When you buy a franchise, you are purchasing a system as much as a business. This is especially true for the bigger and better franchises that provide field-proven instructions to hold your hand through every step of the startup process.

Most big franchisors, for example, choose the specific location for the franchisee's business. They build the outlet, furnish and equip it, staff it, provide the franchisee with the training needed to run the whole thing, and help advertise; they provide everything, soup to nuts.

Smaller franchisors offer fewer services. Any solid small company, however, will still provide a reasonable amount of training, advice, marketing help, and promotional aids. Older, experienced businesspersons who are strong in work skills but weak in organizational ability usually find the ready-made style franchise especially attractive.

Pro Three: You are provided with training, instructions, and guidance from the franchisor.
Even if you choose a franchise that puts your longtime skills to work, there are always new things to learn about a business before you hang out a shingle. One advantage of a franchise is that the franchisor teaches them to you.

Training depends to a large extent on the type of business you're interested in buying. Learning the ropes of, let's say, an inexpensive vending-machine franchise requires only a few days of instruction. Running a Burger King, on the other hand, requires months of instruction and in-the-field practice before a full range of skills is mastered.

As a rule, smaller franchisors provide a short regimen of training that may include training manuals and videos, computer programs, perhaps a day or two of on-site training, and ongoing telephone counseling/support. The larger enterprises offer longer and more comprehensive training sessions. Some even send new recruits to special training facilities. Holiday Inn, for example, maintains a training site known as Holiday Inn University where new franchisees "go back to school" for weeks of intensive instruction.

Once up and running, this help then continues. Ongoing education, refresher courses, new research information, advice hotlines, promotional events, point-of-sale marketing aids, advertising materials, bulk buying from suppliers at competitive or even discount rates—there are many benefits that a franchisor can provide. Many of these aids would normally be unavailable—or unaffordable—to an independent business.

Pro Four: Financial help is often available to the franchisee directly from the franchisor or from the Small Business Administration.

If aspiring franchisees meet the qualifications, financial assistance may be available from a franchisor's personal or private business funds. While this is not the case with every franchisor, it's common practice with many of them, especially when the buy-in price is substantial.

In such cases, franchisors will negotiate a reasonable down payment for the initial investment, and then make arrangements for you to pay off the remainder over an agreed-upon length of time. Or, if you are applying for a bank loan to finance your new business, a franchisor may act as a go-between and a guarantor.

When large sums of money are passing hands the franchisor may also help franchisees work out a payment schedule that does not break their bank, and that is pegged to the franchise's yearly profits. Or again, franchisors may cut their franchisees some financial slack by allowing them to make extended payments for supplies, services, and goods.

Finally, if you're interested in a particular small franchise, check to see if it's listed with the government's Small Business Administration ("small business" meaning that a company has a net worth of less than 7 million dollars).

> You can access the Small Business Administration (SBA) online at *www.sba.gov*. Their website is a goldmine of information and hands-on advice for franchisees. Help is provided by the SBA on obtaining surety bonds and equity capital; receiving online training, counseling, and assistance; and finding information on how to file for a loan. Fill out the application box on this site to obtain their *Finance Primer: Guide to SBA's Loan Guarantee Programs*.

If the franchise company is listed in the SBA's registry, this means, first, that the SBA has scrutinized the company and deems it legit and fair to its franchisees. That's a big plus. Second, if the business is listed in the SBA's registry, you may qualify for the SBA's 7(a) Loan Program that provides seventy-five percent guaranties on low-interest loans of up to 2 million dollars. These loans are designed to serve small businesses that don't qualify for loans through conventional lending channels. Once received from the SBA, this money can be applied to any sector of your business plan that you prefer: construction, equipment, inventory, and/or marketing. Obviously, this is another huge bonus.

Finally, remember that any on-the-ball franchisor will be cheering for you to succeed because when you succeed, they succeed. If they like your stats and style, and if they want you in their stable, one way or another they'll make sure you get the investment capital you need.

Pro Five: The franchisor will help you market and promote your business.
This is part of the turnkey deal. When you buy a franchise, you automatically acquire the right to use the franchisor's brand name, trademark, signage, advertising, tested operating systems, and other identifiable features such as a logo or a branded style of architecture (think of the McDonald's arches or the slanting orange roofs on the old Howard Johnson's).

Needless to say, product identification is a benefit exclusive to large, high-recognition companies. By way of compensation, many small and mid-sized franchisors provide advertising aids, marketing tools, site selection resources, and promotional ideas. When looking into the purchase of a franchise, be sure to ask about the selling aids that the franchise offers.

Those are some of the major pros. Now for the major cons—as in "contraindications," not as in "con men."

Con One: You must pay the franchise fee plus assorted startup costs.
Perhaps it's unfair to label this as a "con." Paying one's dues might be a better term.

There are, of course, extremely inexpensive franchises for sale in the marketplace, and you could get lucky. By and large though, you get what you pay for. Realistically speaking, $30,000 to $50,000 is the minimum price for a franchise that provides some brand name clout plus a time-proven operating system.

But be prepared; the initial outlay doesn't end here. Other startup expenses can include legal fees, construction costs, decor, equipment, inventory, supplies, transportation, labor, promotion, a two to five percent advertising fee if the company promotes its product nationally, not to mention endless incidentals. Franchise experts will advise you to stock a six- or eight-month liquid reserve fund to cover all unanticipated costs, personal expenses, and emergencies.

Con Two: You will no longer be independent.
It's not much of a reach to say that, from a business point of view, the franchisor owns the franchisee lock, stock, and barrel. This, at least, is true for large established franchisors that apply ironclad managerial, promotional, design, and financial formulas to their chain franchises.

We've already seen these large franchisors in action. They tell you where your business should be located, whom you should hire, how much money to charge, what to put in your windows, when to take your vacations, yada, yada, yada.

Whether you're cool with this degree of control or not is a matter of personality.

For fifty-plus entrepreneurs accustomed to making their own command line decisions and running their own show, a highly regulated franchise can possibly be an unwise choice. Those who work well under close management and who are comfortable leaving the big decisions to higher ups will find this con to be more like a pro.

Con Three: Every month, you must pay a percent of your earnings to the franchisor.
Besides the price of admission, franchisors expect you to pay them monthly royalties. This rendering unto Caesar can get old pretty quick. You've already sunk a lot of money into buying the franchise. Now they want more—forever.

In this regard, watch out for franchisors that continually pressure franchisees to increase their profits and hence pay larger monthly percentage fees. All the franchisor is interested in is volume, volume, and volume. This push-me, pull-you impasse can get sticky for both parties, and sometimes make for bad blood.

Thus, when researching the franchise, be sure to ask other franchisees if they've run into problems of this sort. If the franchisor won't let you talk to its other franchisees, consider this a very bad sign, perhaps even a deal breaker.

Con Four: You are legally bound to the terms of your contract.

The moment you sign your name to the contract, you are legally obliged to abide by the franchisor's rules and regulations. This means that if your business does not show a profit quickly enough, or if it simply turns out to be a lemon, you may be chained to the terms of your agreement with no way out.

In such cases, people find themselves slaves to the machine, working at a job they dislike, in a business that doesn't work, and, adding insult to injury, that scarcely pays a living wage. We know of one case wherein a middle-aged woman left her job as a stenographer and bought a credit repair franchise. She soon discovered that the company was unresponsive and disreputable, but she was tied up in an exploitive contract that she had not taken the time to read carefully (and had not shown to a lawyer) and from which she was unable to legally extricate herself. She ended up laboring at her franchise business during the day to break even and working a second job at night to pay for the groceries.

Avoid such traps at the beginning by reading the contract carefully and by seeking the advice of professionals who know the franchise ropes. Even for fifty-plus workers who've been part of the business world for years caution is advised; franchises are different animals from other types of businesses. They have their own ground rules and their own legal twists and turns. They should always be approached with eyes wide open.

Con Five: Your success is tied to the success of the franchisor and to its other franchises.

Do the math. If one or more of the outlets in your franchise performs badly, this affects the reputation and, consequently, the profits of all the other outlets—including yours. The truth is, for better or for worse, you are joined at the hip to your brother and sister franchises. Or, consider another scenario: The franchisor mismanages its business into the ground. You and the other chains are left holding the bag. Everyone loses.

These are calculated risks, of course, as in any business. But they are risks unique to the franchise world. A franchisor is like a boat, and its franchises are its passengers. If the boat springs a leak, all the passengers get wet. If the boat sinks, more often than not, the passengers all go down with it.

Of course, if things fall apart financially, and you're young and resilient, there's always tomorrow. But if you are older, and if you have put your hard-earned savings into a franchise that fails, the options for recovery are more limited.

Lesson?

Go with a franchisor that has been around for a while, that is a proven success with the public, that's known for its fair practices, and that has an attractive financial track record. Going this route will cost you more, most likely. But look at the extra expense as insurance on your investment. In the long run, paying more for a known winner will substantially improve your odds of success.

RESEARCH COUNTS: A FRANCHISEE CASE STUDY

Profile—At age fifty-four Gene Wayne had built, by anyone's standards, a terrific career. After earning an MBA in Finance from George Washington University, he started working at the George Washington University Hospital as a business manager. He then took several positions at various health institutions, eventually becoming vice president of an 18-hospital chain where he was responsible for financial and informational technology. Before he was fifty he was CEO of the Eugenia Hospital System with its four locations and 70,000 patients.

In his fifties, Gene started to grow restless. He began craving a more entrepreneurial type of career, one that involved physical work and hands-on creativity. Being a gourmet cook, he thought about the restaurant business, but rejected it because it was too labor intensive, and because he wanted to spend more time with his family. Poring over the Opportunity section of the newspaper one day, he saw a two-line advertisement for a handyman business, Handyman Matters. Gene had always been an amateur house restorer, owning several old houses and fixing them up for sale. He called the number in the ad and reached the owner of the local franchise, a business that focused on small to medium sized house restoration and repair jobs.

The current owner was struggling with the business, Gene learned. So to ensure that he didn't make a fatal mistake, he decided to perform his own due diligence.

He began by reviewing all client records and every expense the business had incurred. He studied the types of jobs the franchise was taking on at the time and analyzed how much it received in fees from each commission.

He also studied the area demographics. How many people lived in his perspective franchise area? What was the general income and educational level? What types of houses were most popular? What was the average age of local houses, and what were they worth on the market?

Gene also checked out the people who worked at the Handyman Matters franchise head office. After several conversations he decided they were competent. He also liked them personally, and trusted them. They passed his "chemistry test." When Gene completed his due diligence he concluded that this company could, in fact, be profitable.

He also saw the pluses of buying an existing franchise. He wouldn't have to wait for the Yellow Pages and Internet listings to come out. He already had a customer base, plus necessary marketing materials such as brochures and business cards. He negotiated to buy the existing franchise for $30,000, and was soon in business for himself.

Based on this research, he estimated how much the business would make if he ran it. Based on those estimates, Gene made a deal to buy the existing franchise for about the same as a new franchise—about $30,000. Now in his third year, Gene has six full-time employees he calls "craftsmen." Gene never subcontracts out his jobs. If he or his staff can't do the work, he refers customers to someone who can. This is his version of quality control. He is also optimistic about the future, so much so that he has purchased the franchise for his adjoining territory, doubling the potential size of his business.

Besides the purchase of the franchise territory, Handyman Matters franchisees pay about six percent of their revenues to the franchisor. Gene feels this somewhat high cost is worth it. The company has a computer system that he's allowed to use, and that helps him estimate jobs and track payments. The company also provides him with marketing materials, advertising, and estimating tools.

Gene feels that his connection to Handyman Matters is a good fit, and that the franchisor-franchisee partnership is mutually beneficial. His current goal is to grow his franchise and eventually sell it for a profit. All in all, he thinks, he found himself a pretty good deal.

How to choose a franchise that's right for your needs

What basic things should you do and not do when choosing a franchise? The following six pieces of advice will get you started:

1. Focus only on the types of businesses you are interested in.

If automobiles are your passion, look for car- or truck-related businesses. If you've always dreamed of running a restaurant, consider a food-related franchise. If you have accounting skills, a tax-preparation franchise may well suit your needs. The main thing is to avoid wasting time investigating franchises that don't capture your fancy.

Best advice: Go with your established interests, skills, and satisfactions, then narrow down the choices and zero in on the two or three franchises in these areas that have the greatest appeal.

Then learn all you can about them.

2. Research, research, research.

Research may well be the most important step you'll take on the road to finding a compatible franchise. Take your time here, and learn all you can. Rushing into a franchise purchase on impulse, whim, or hearsay is a sure recipe for mishap.

When you do find a company that interests you, start by reading their Uniform Franchise Offering Circular (UFOC), a document that every franchisor is obliged by federal law to provide before any deal can be made.

In this three-part document, you will find:
1. A set of the franchisor's audited financial statements
2. A copy of their standard contract
3. Information on twenty-three fundamental topics covering all aspects of the franchisor's business operations

Among these twenty-three subjects are disclosure clauses on the company's business experience, their franchise fee and initial costs, their financing agreements, their financial statements, their projected sales and earnings, their renewal and termination agreements, the obligations of the franchisee to the franchisor, and more.

Source list for finding help and advice when buying a franchise

- American Association of Franchisees and Dealers (AAFD), PO Box 81887, San Diego. CA 92138, 800-733-9858 (trade organization dedicated to helping both franchisors and franchisees)
- American Marketing Association, 250 S. Wacker Drive, Suite 200, Chicago, IL 60606, 312-648-0536 (a solid franchise marketing resource)
- *www.franchisetimes.com* (a subscription service that offers a hefty amount of valuable franchising information)
- FranNet, *www.frannet.com* (a franchise broker that helps assess and select franchises for franchisees)
- International Franchise Association (IFA), 1350 New York Avenue, NW, Suite 900, Washington, D.C. 20005, 202-662-0763 (the largest trade organization dedicated to franchising in the United States)
- U.S. Franchise News, *www.usfranchisenews.com* (extensive web-based source for franchise information)

Read these twenty-three topics carefully, compiling a list of questions and comments as you go. If you find the language too dense or technical, hire a lawyer or franchise broker to advise you. For many people, misreading or misinterpreting a franchisor's legal material at the beginning opens a Pandora's Box of financial and legal problems that come back later to haunt them. So be *sure* you are clear on all contractual points from the start. Remember, the money you pay a franchise professional up front can save you a thousand times this amount down the line.

Meanwhile—and this is really important—visit one or more of the franchise's locations and talk to several veteran franchisees. Ask them the hard questions: Is the business viable? Is the franchisee making a profit? If not, why not? And when, if ever, does the franchisee foresee financial success? Is the franchisor fair and honest? Does it meet all its obligations? Has it provided the franchisee with everything it promised at the beginning? Does it provide adequate promotion and ongoing support? What are particular complications or problems to be aware of? What mistakes can you avoid making? All in all, does the franchisee recommend the franchisor?

No one is going to know more about the franchisor than its franchisees. Speak to them on the phone or, better, in person. The conversations that ensue may well be the deal maker or the deal breaker. As the saying goes, "ask the patient, not the doctor."

If you're still enthusiastic about the franchise after you've read their UFOC and talked to other franchisees, now is the time to meet directly with the officers and managers that run the company. Some prospective buyers bring a lawyer to these sessions to help interpret technical issues and to ask the franchisor questions they themselves may not think of.

Another bit of sound policy at the research stage is to study all relevant printed and online materials.

For example, *Bond's Franchise Guide* offers data on thousands of American franchises, along with helpful franchising facts and advice. You can purchase it from Bond's website at *www.worldfranchising.com*. *Franchise Opportunities Guide*, published by the International Franchise Association, is useful, too, with plenty of information on all aspects of franchise evaluation and purchase. Buy it on *www.franchise.org*.

Also, check out the hefty list of books published by Franchise Update Publications. It's on their website at *www.Franchise-Update.com*.

Finally, take a holistic approach to your fact-finding mission. Poke around as much you can. Talk to people in the industry. Visit franchise expositions and trade shows (the biggest are held in Los Angeles; Washington, D.C.; and Miami). Look for relevant—and revealing—data online. Read the trade journals.

Then put it all together and you should have a reasonably clear picture of the pros and cons of the franchises in which you're interested.

3. Be clear on their policies, as well as the services that are provided (and not provided) by the franchisor.

A sample checklist includes:
- Does the franchisor offer startup loans, or will it help you acquire a loan? Will it provide further loans and assistance if your new franchise founders?
- If you plan to build your franchise location from scratch, does the franchisor provide help with choice of building site, architectural blueprints, construction, labor, exterior design, interior decor, landscaping, and other get-started aids? How much of these construction costs are covered in the franchise price? How much, if any, must come out of your own pocket?
- How strong is the demand for the franchisor's product or services in your neighborhood? Is the product or service offered location-specific, or can it be sold and promoted anywhere? You would not, we assume, want to open a ribs and chops restaurant on a block populated entirely by vegans.
- Is there any chance that the services offered by the franchisor will become outdated or irrelevant within the next five to ten years? This happens most commonly in the electronics field where new advances are constantly obsolescing yesterday's highly touted widget. Think, for instance, of the people who invested in fast 35mm film development franchises. Digital cameras came along and wiped them out. Buyer beware.
- How close is the nearest competitor franchise to your new location? If you plan to purchase a Fat Boy Burger House, you certainly don't want another Fat Boy two blocks—or a

two-minute drive—up the street from you. Be sure to ask the franchisor what their policy is concerning minimum distance between franchises.

- What type of training does the franchisor provide? How many days or weeks does the training period last? Is the training ongoing, with periodic sessions that provide new information and refresher courses? Does the company include training in marketing, advertising, staff management, safety, and technical operations?
- Does the franchisor offer advice and sources for purchasing equipment, inventory, and supplies? Will it arrange for you to purchase these items at a bulk discount?
- What type of marketing tools and advice does the franchisor offer?
- If necessary, does the franchisor provide periodic updates to your decor to help you stay current?
- How computerized is the franchise operation? Does the franchisor offer proprietary software of any kind? If needed, how much computer training is provided? Is tech assistance available from the franchisor? Does the franchisor have a website? Will it add you to its site and/or help you construct your own?
- What type of local or national advertising does the franchisor provide, if any? What must you pay to use these services? Are the company's advertising promotions ongoing or time-limited? *Must* you use (and pay for) the franchisor's advertising? Or can you do advertising and promotion on your own?
- Does the franchisor sponsor special events, promotions, conferences, conventions, or regional meetings? How often? What kinds?

FRANCHISEE CASE STUDY: PULLING ITS WEIGHT

Profile—Alan Winter worked as an executive in the garment industry for almost thirty years, running companies for some of the leading manufacturers in the business. When the industry started to shrink, however, he decided it was time to seek greener pastures.

Trouble was, opportunities in the garment business were shrinking along with demand, and worse, his age now made him less attractive to potential employers.

So Alan started looking at franchises—everything from yogurt shops to dry cleaning. He rejected all these, hoping instead to find a service-oriented business.

Finally he came across a franchise known as Caring Transitions. This small (but not too small) company helped older people manage the transition of moving from a long time home to a retirement care facility. Caring Transitions provided services such as sorting through belongings, documenting family history, selling unwanted items, running yard sales, cleaning homes, and running errands.

The franchise cost $22,000, including fees of six percent of revenues. Today this is all fine with Alan, who feels the franchisor really delivers value in the form of national brand, marketing materials, marketing strategies, and professional advice, all of which are provided in liberal portions.

After six months Alan's franchise is not yet profitable. But the signs are encouraging, he insists, and he is optimistic about the future. Most importantly, he is pleased with his franchise and feels it is definitely pulling its own weight. "When a franchisor is cooperative and obliging," he tells us, "that's more than half the battle."

4. Decide if you want to purchase a new or already existing franchise location.

Both options have their advantages and disadvantages.

Buying a franchise from scratch means you must finance all preparations for startup and build-out. The list of possible costs can be intimidating: construction, labor, new equipment, professional fees, plus a list as long as your arm for design and decoration. Some of these costs will be covered in the franchise price, and some won't. Find out how all this works at the beginning.

What are the advantages of establishing your own business? By starting from scratch, you get a virgin site, a new plant, new equipment, and a business that you have, in a manner of speaking, birthed yourself.

Existing franchises, on the other hand, offer an up-and-running operation with a ready-made clientele. The equipment is already in place, the staff is at work, and, assuming that this franchise has passed its breakeven point, you have access to immediate cash flow.

However, be sure an established up-and-running outlet has a good reputation and a solid customer base. Check to see if the plant and equipment are in good condition (many are not), and that the business is, in fact, making money. The franchisor's UFOC will offer some form of financial records profiling its past three- or four-year performance. If these records are inadequate, ask to see more. Also, check the lease and look at the status of the license terms with the franchisor. If the agreement period is drawing to a close and has only three years left on a fifteen-year term, this franchise is a good deal less viable and valuable than one that has eight to ten more years.

5. Make sure you have a comprehensive knowledge of the costs involved in purchasing and running the franchise.

The bottom line makes the world go 'round in the franchising industry.

Nothing new here. Still, it's vital—*vital*—that you approach a franchise purchase armed with detailed knowledge of all its expenses. As far as you can determine, what is the *total* investment necessary for buying the franchise and getting it off the ground? Do you have access to all this needed capital *plus* a well-padded cushion for those inevitable financial surprises? What type of earning projections does the franchisor offer, if any? How much can you afford to lose if the venture goes south?

Don't try to ballpark your financials. Be as precise as you can about both individual and total costs. This information should be carefully spelled out in your business plan.

As any franchise broker, lawyer, or accountant will tell you, the reason most franchises go out of business is undercapitalization. This situation results most commonly from poor planning, especially the underestimation of—and lack of knowledge concerning—the full range of startup expenditures for a particular franchise. So be painfully honest with yourself in the numbers department. Even better, seek the help of franchise professionals to help you compute the costs of starting your franchise, many of which (such as legal fees, insurance, taxes, zoning expenses, landscaping, maintenance, repairs, transportation, and/or travel) may not be immediately apparent.

6. A number of franchise funding sources are available. Check them out.

As we've learned, many franchisors offer franchisees financial assistance. That's one prime source.

Another is the federal government.

The Small Business Administration's 7(a) loans are especially popular for financing small franchise purchases, as well as for gaining working capital and acquiring new (or better) equipment. Lowdoc loans (standing for "low documentation," which means just what you think it does) are fast, under-$100,000 financing aids that can be obtained from mortgage brokers. The CDC/504 loan program is a long-term financing tool especially designed to help small businesses. It is used for acquiring fixed assets such as land or the construction of a new facility. The CDC/504 loan works through the SBA. In many states, local government agencies will finance small franchise loans. Check with your nearest Chamber of Commerce for details. For a good overview of small business loans, check out *www.proposalwriter.com/govtloans.html.*

Other funding sources include commercial banks, credit unions, and savings and loan associations. Don't forget home equity loans, too. Money may also be available from large private lenders like G.E. Financial, The Money Store, and AT&T Small Business Lending Corporation. Finally, there's the personal route: friends, business associations, and family members.

It's a pretty wide selection, and somewhere in the mix you're likely to find the money you need. Just cover all the bases—and be persistent.

7. If you're seeking outside financing you'll need a business plan.

Whichever person or institution you approach for money to capitalize your franchise, 999 times out of a thousand they'll expect to see a full business plan.

Investors will ask how your franchise works from an operational, managerial, marketing, and financial perspective. They'll want to know how well suited you are to run it, how you'll spend the money they lend you, when and how you intend to repay it, and what type of monetary returns they can hope to see down the road.

It's a bit of work. But keep in mind that a well-done business plan assists you as much as it helps the lender and the franchisor, and it's a strong selling tool, too. It helps you get organized and focused and provides a three-dimensional map of the monetary, operational, and managerial issues you'll need to know to get your business off the ground. If done properly, it forces you to take a hard look at both the big picture and the small-print business details, and in the process, it helps you make an objective evaluation of your earning potential and chances of financial success.

Although providing detailed instructions for creating a franchise business plan is beyond the scope of this book, here's a down-and-dirty summary of its key sections:

1. An overall description of the franchise: What it sells, its location, its competition, its management, and its market.
2. A description of the contract that exists between you and the franchisor.
3. A detailed financial breakdown of the sources of funding, income and cash flow projections; the costs of equipment, salaries, and suppliers; and balance sheets for existing franchises.
4. Supporting documents: References, recommendations, awards, personal financial statements, lease agreements, supplier contracts, and résumés.

If you're practiced at writing a business plan, go for it. If not, seek assistance from an accountant or lawyer who is well versed in franchise matters. Your business plan will make or break your chances of getting the money you need. You'll definitely want to get this one right from the start.

Franchising choices and concerns for the fifty-plus entrepreneur

So much for how franchising works. The question now is how well will it work for *you*—for your current ambitions, age, financial resources, family life, and personal goals?

Here are some steps to take and questions to ask to help you figure it out:

- **How much money do you want to earn at this time in your life? How much are you prepared to risk?**—These two questions have popped up in previous chapters. They are especially relevant for fifty-plus franchisees. Assume, for example, that you've spent a lifetime working and saving. You've acquired a handsome, or at least a well-padded nest egg. Just how protected is this nest egg? What percent of its funds can spiral down the drain on a failed franchise enterprise and still leave you financially healthy?

    Or, if things go swimmingly, will you still make the amount of money you're accustomed to earning at the old nine-to-five job? Will it be enough to live on after the startup blood, sweat, and tears are spilled? Even if you're investing in a proven and developed business concept with high income potential, things can go wrong—sometimes very wrong. Life is full of risk. Are you willing to take it? As they say at the tables in Las Vegas: How much of your money can you afford to lose?

    "Later in life is not the time to shoot craps and risk your financial security," an Ask Annie article warns us in an October 12, 2006, issue of *Fortune* magazine. "It's worth sitting down with a reputable accountant who has worked with lots of startups, and who can help you determine how much of a gamble you're willing and able to take."

    This is a lesson worth taking to heart. Conferring with knowledgeable associates and friends or with a financial professional is always good medicine. Also, check out the "Is Franchising for Me" workbook on the Small Business Administration's website at *www.sba.gov*. The Federal Trade Commission's on-line report, "A Consumer Guide to Buying

a Franchise," will also give you food for thought. It's at *www.ftc.gov*.
- **Personal Goals**—The question to ask is not just "Do I want to own a franchise?" but "Which franchise best fits my lifestyle requirements?"

    This question boils down to a matter of personal goals. Do you intend to work out of your home or at an outside office? Plan accordingly. Do you lean toward a franchise that involves other family members, or are you a solo act? Are you most comfortable spending your middle and later years operating a full-time, labor-intensive franchise with, presumably, high profit rewards, or do you prefer a work-when-I-want-to, earn-some-extra money-on-the-side kind of concern?

    Or again, perhaps an "earn as you sleep" business is your thing; that is, an investment franchise in which you buy into a chain, then hire one or more people to run it for you, freeing up your time and energy for other pursuits.

    There is no right or wrong answer here. Just the need for some judicious decision-making. Certain fifty-plus entrepreneurs get their pleasure from long hours at work; others prefer the easy-does-it approach. Ask yourself: How many days a week do I want to work for the rest of my life? Some franchises, especially the less expensive ones (and usually, it should be added, the lower earning ones), set you up at home where you can work at your own pace. This easy-does-it approach allows you to make your own hours, vacation when you like, and be more of your own boss. Other franchises are twenty-four/seven operations that demand constant hard work and that have strict controls over your time but also deliver large profits to match. Weigh and consider.
- **Make use of the networks you've established over the years**—If you intend to purchase a franchise and need all the good advice you can get, now is the time to dig into your old Rolodex, written and electronic. Fortunately, you enter the game here with a clear advantage. Most workplace veterans have developed business relationships of one kind or

another with large numbers of individuals. These contacts can really help. Think work associates: colleagues, bankers, accountants, lawyers, managers, executives, financiers, advertisers, teachers, students, and tech people. Ask yourself: With whom have you crossed paths over the years that knows about franchising? Who has helped you before? Who owes you? Who likes you? Who among your many past business associates can now give you genuine and sympathetic help?

The seven basic supports that over-fifty franchisors most commonly need:

1. Investors and sources of capital
2. A good business plan
3. Careful market research
4. Expert council
5. IT and computer training
6. A network built of past business and financial contacts
7. Ongoing business mentoring

- **Age**—Franchises are demanding critters, especially at the beginning when there are hundreds of things to learn, build, carry, deliver, stay on top of; *plus* hundreds of nice and not-so-nice people to deal with; *plus* hundreds—make that thousands—of details and demands. So if you do plan to purchase a franchise, think about choosing a business that best fits your age-related needs.

    For example, if you are fifty-seven years old and in good health, the odds are that you can easily handle a labor-intensive franchise that demands hard physical work or constant travel. At age seventy-seven, the view is somewhat different, both in terms of energy level and in number of years you wish to stay with this job. In the latter case, consider a franchise that is centered on deskwork or one that requires limited hours a week to run.

    It's your choice, needless to say, and if the spirit is willing at whatever age, the sky's the limit. On the other hand, realities are realities. Choose carefully on this one.

- **Health**—This is the same as above but more specifically body centered. Are you in good physical shape? Do you workout and keep fit? How deep does your hour-to-hour energy pool go? Do you tire easily? Does your mind stop working clearly after a few hours in the office? Do you have any physical challenges? How many hours a day does your stamina level comfortably endure? Are you on strong or enervating medication?

    For people suffering from a chronic ailment of one kind or another, or for those whose body parts don't work as well as they once did, a sedentary business close to home may be the wisest choice. Of course, if you're on top of your physical game, then no worries. Still, a word of caution: You do not want to spend your savings on a franchise and then discover that for one physical reason or another you're not up to running it. Be sure, therefore, that you are well insured when entering your new career, and that your business ambitions do not outrun your common sense.

- **Past experience versus new learning challenges**—Many franchisors make a great deal of hoopla over the fact that no experience is required to run their show. But is this necessarily a good thing? You've spent years working at a chosen profession, and now you want to move on to greener pastures. Or, maybe you don't. For many fifty-plus entrepreneurs, a franchise involving skills they've honed over a lifetime is just what the doctor ordered. An unfamiliar profession requires lots of training and a steep learning curve. Some people don't want to spend the time and effort, but others do. In fact, it's what they're looking for at this stage of life: new dragons to slay.

    Bottom line? See the issue from both sides, evaluate it from your personal perspective, and then decide.

- **Gauge your technology skills**—Most members of the fifty-plus generation are quite comfortable using computers and its large family of chip-based offspring, but not all of us. If you are a computerphobe, or if you just don't cotton to the click and hum of twenty-first-century office machinery all day long, choose a franchise that's low-tech or no-tech.

- **Time concerns**—How many hours a day do you want to spend working at your franchise? Many? Few? As opposed to time spent playing tennis or cards or chess? Time spent gardening, laying brick, going to the mall and to the movies? Time spent taking photographs, learning a language, hanging out with friends, building dollhouses or kitchen cabinets, volunteering for charity, playing with grandchildren, visiting your club or organization, going back to school, taking care of family members, traveling cross country or to foreign climes? Whatever your pleasures and duties happen to be, factor them all in, then choose the franchise with hours and demands that best suit your schedule.
- **Family**—If your elderly mother is needy and requires care, this will be a primary concern when choosing franchise opportunities. If you have teenage children at home or grandchildren, how much care and supervision do they require? How much time will be left over to run the franchise?

    As far as the plusses and minuses of a family franchise go, on the positive side, there's the fact that when you pay a family member, this salary is deductible as a business expense. The money stays in the family. The head of a family franchise also gets to use before-tax dollars to pay other family members, a neat perk that's actually a kind of hidden tax shelter. Also, a family franchise can serve as a business training ground for younger family members as well as an ongoing source of family income after the death or retirement of the senior member—you.

    Finally, in a family business you will be working with people you know and love. That's a big benefit. Keep in mind, though, that every stick has two ends. Sometimes this very familiarity lights short fuses, causing financial and managerial disagreements today, family feuds tomorrow. And when the members of a family franchise cannot see eye-to-eye, sibling rivalries can flare, marital disputes escalate, and old wounds between parent and child open up wider than ever before.

    There's no precise way to gauge how well your particular family will work together as a business group. Still, there are ways to lay a strong foundation. Ask each other the hard questions. Talk through financial and operational matters as a family unit before beginning. Make sure the power structure of your business is set and agreed upon by everyone beforehand and that all family members in the business know exactly where they stand. Then act accordingly. The next chapter deals in depth with family and fifty-plus entrepreneurship.

- **Exit strategies**—You may wish to work at a franchise for five years, say, and then retire. Or you may want to labor hard for a certain number of years, earn lots of money, then get out and do something else. You may even get bored running the franchise and feel the urge to move on, or you may simply want to start another business.

  The important thing is to coordinate the length of your franchise contract to your age, your financial situation, and your general inclination to remain working in this particular profession.

  Remember, the length of time a contract runs can range from five to twenty years. At the end of this appointed time, assuming you want to keep at it, you must then renegotiate the contract with the franchisor, sometimes paying a renewal or successor fee. Advanced planning and knowledge is therefore the watchword here. Know how many years your contract extends. Find out what your termination rights are. Sometimes eager franchisors are willing to negotiate with you on this and other termination issues, even offering you an out clause should you become ill or wish to start another business.

  Finally, be clear on all renewal costs and obligations before you sign the contract. And if you're thinking of passing down the franchise to your children, find out what provisions the franchisor makes for this situation. Being well informed at the beginning of a business enterprise can save you lots of time, lots of dollars, and lots aggravation in the years that follow.

Chapter 8
Fifty-Plus Business—Plus Family

Tricky business

You've reached a certain age. You have a certain amount of experience and investment power under your belt. Now you're anxious to explore new career horizons and go into business for yourself.

It's the same scenario we've seen throughout this book. This time with a twist: You'd like to make this new business a family affair.

Perhaps you have your heart set on starting a new career with one of your children or with your spouse; or with both your spouse and child; or with your niece, brother, sister, cousin, aunt; or with an extended family member, like a daughter-in-law or a stepchild. One big happy family business.

Perhaps you intend to develop a business *for* your children or grandchildren. The plan is, you get the business financed, the relatives come on board, and after a certain number of years working together, they take over and keep the business running, hopefully handing it down themselves to the next generation.

There are an endless number of casting arrangements with which to staff a family-oriented business. Beneath all of them, however, run two inevitable bottom lines, two concerns that underlie—and sometime undermine—every family business:

1. Getting the business to work well and to prosper; and

2. Keeping family relationships within the business on an even and amiable keel.

This second concern is the key element that makes a family business different from all other for-profit enterprises and is the main topic of this chapter. A family business is about economics, yes; but unlike a non-family business, it's also about blood and trust and lifetime relationships—personal DNA connections that are simply not present in any other type of commercial setup.

Look at how the wheels of a non-family business turn.

First of all, in a non-family business, you hire people for their skills and talents. Period. If they don't get the job done your way, you show them the highway. In a non-family business you're the boss. None of your employees is likely to try to steal your thunder, and if they do, you remain judge and jury. In a non-family business, you're interested in profits first and in the happiness of your employees second (or third, or fourth). In a non-family business, you provide employees with whatever benefits you can afford. If your employees are not satisfied with the deal, they are free to leave.

In a family business, the ground rules run along considerably different lines.

If your workers also happen to be a daughter or a brother or a spouse, you automatically have an emotional relationship with them as well as a financial one. Unless you're made of steel, it becomes seriously difficult to fire family members, refuse to hire them to begin with, turn a deaf ear to their salary needs, ignore them when they have bright ideas, or deny an employed child (who also happens to be raising your two grandchildren) health benefits.

So face it, there is simply no way to entirely separate your personal feelings from the business decisions you must make with family members. To have a family business is to a have a business that is all about family.

What makes or breaks a family business?

Traditionally speaking, a family business involves at least two family members. This pair (or trio or foursome) is usually constituted of close relatives such as a husband and wife, two sisters, or three brothers, all of whom participate in the daily workings of the business.

In a family dry cleaning operation, for example, the mother may deal with customers at the front desk while the father oversees the employees and maintains the machines. A son living nearby keeps the books, a granddaughter delivers the pressed clothes to customers' homes every day after school, and a grandmother writes and sends out advertising mailings.

Most family businesses tend to be small and to focus on retail and service-oriented ventures. Many have a history that goes back a generation or two. In the case of a fifty-plus startup, besides making a profit for all involved, generational aims include establishing long-term employment opportunities for one's children, or generating an annuity that can be passed on to one's spouse in case of disability or death.

Most of all, a family business has specific advantages and disadvantages that separate it from other forms of business.

On the positive side, a family business makes it possible for you to spend more time with your spouse and children, an asset that is especially appreciated if you've worked nine-to-five for years to the constant complaints of family members that you're never home.

A family business helps you provide relatives with the kind of career and profit-making opportunities they might otherwise never realize. It allows you to work with associates you trust, who are loyal, who are willing to make sacrifices for the good of the company—people with whom you're comfortable and who care about you, people that you're happy to brush shoulders with every day and whom you are proud to see grow and prosper on the job. And, of course, a family business helps you create an enduring commercial enterprise that can then be passed on to younger family members.

Those are the major perks.

Meanwhile, on the debit side is the fact that when running a family concern, you are often obliged to manage personal issues that can be confusing, contentious, and that have a long emotional history reaching far back into the family's past. You must deal with the kind of constraints and complications that would not ordinarily show their heads in a non-family business environment.

Say, for example, that you and your middle-aged sister start an accounting firm together. She's worked as a bookkeeper for several small companies, and seems to know her stuff. After working side by side for a year, however, it becomes devastatingly clear that sis would have been more of an asset to the family name if she'd kept her day job. She's grossly incompetent.

Yet you can't fire her. She's a partner. And more to the point, she's *your sister*.

At the same time, it's obvious to everyone that she is running the business into the ground.

Another scenario is that you start a business with your husband and your brother. Your husband feels that he does a great deal more of the heavy lifting in the workplace than your brother, and he resents the fact that your brother receives a full one-third of the profits. Your brother should get no more than twenty-five percent, your husband insists; but your brother thinks quite differently on the matter. Soon there's no love lost between the two rivals. You're caught in the middle without a conflict-free option.

Or, say two wealthy relatives put up money for your new gift shop while you and your niece run the business day to day. As far as your rich relatives are concerned, their investment is strictly a dollars-and-cents deal. If after a few years profits are not rolling in, they may start hectoring you to sell the store. For you and your niece, however, the store has become both life and livelihood. You've put everything you have into it and are deeply invested. Your rich relatives simply don't understand. "Ah, but we do," they reply. "You took our money, you spent it, and now, two years later, we're not receiving the promised returns. Therefore, it's time to sell this loser business and move on."

Result: Possible financial peril, possible litigation, and guaranteed dagger-filled atmosphere at the Thanksgiving table every year.

The six important points to remember when starting a fifty-plus family business

If you intend to start a family business with yourself in the role of fifty-plus workplace veteran and various relatives as partners and employees, you have a mandate to minimize the problems associated with family businesses and to maximize the benefits from the start.

How?

The short answer is: With careful and intelligent advance planning.

Here are six steps you can take to build a solid and relatively bulletproof family business structure from the very beginning:

1. Choose family employees realistically and objectively.

Although family is all about feelings and relationships, in a family business, sentimentality should have little or no place. Assuming that you want your new enterprise to succeed, it is vital that you staff it with family members whom you know are trustworthy, efficient, hardworking, and up to the task.

True, your nephew Larry is smart and talented, and he *really* needs a job—but he is also belligerent, lazy, and has a record of walking away from high-paying jobs. Although his mother, your sister, is begging you to hire him, do you really want a flake like Larry as your right-hand man?

And true, your wife has her heart set on working at the front desk of your new bed-and-breakfast, dealing with paying guests all day long. But is this such a great idea, given her not-so-terrific social skills? Mightn't she be better used in the back room where her bookkeeping talents can profit everyone?

Then there's the opposite case. Having studied martial arts most of your life, you've opened a martial arts studio under the assumption that your daughter, a third-degree black belt, will help you run it. But when you ask her to come on board, you discover that she has other plans. Meanwhile, you've been banking on her partnership from the start. In fact, you would not have gone to all this trouble, you tell her, if you'd known she would take a job elsewhere.

"But I never said I was *definitely* interested!" your daughter replies. "And stop guilt-tripping me!"

"But you specifically said it would be great if we could work together teaching martial arts!" you retort.

"That wasn't a *promise*," she replies. "It was just a thought."

The argument goes on.

Moral? Never assume. Be certain of your assets from the start.

2. Develop a full operational strategy.

Don't wing it.

Have a business plan that not only organizes and defines your new business, but that carefully spells out the role, job description, and financial distributions for every family employee.

Make it official. Have a lawyer draw up the contracts. Work with an accountant if necessary or a tax planner on partnership agreements. If you're looking for investment capital, hire a professional to help you develop a first-rate business plan. Be sure that family employees know where they fit into the company and what their rights, obligations, and limitations consist of. Make sure everything is in writing and on the books.

3. Establish an agreed-upon authority structure from the start.

In a non-family enterprise, the boss is the boss is the boss. His or her word is law.

In a family-based business, the boss may be the boss all right, but his or her "employees"—read: son, daughter, nephew, granddaughter, etc.—often feel empowered to challenge policy and decisions by right of blood alone.

Subtle problems of all kinds can arise. For example, if you manage your own business and a crisis occurs, are you still beholden to old Uncle Harry, who, though not part of your business proper, traditionally makes all the big decisions in your family? If you're in business with brothers Ted and Mike with whom you've been intensely competitive since you were kids, you can bank on a power struggle every time a major decision must be made. It will remain this way *unless* you establish an agreed-upon chain of command at the inception.

There are ways to avoid these pitfalls.

For example, you as founder of the company may want to create a board of directors that is staffed by family and non-family members alike. It is understood from the start that this committee works under you, handles all secondary issues, and develops policy and strategy, but it ultimately defers to you on final judgments.

Some family businesses employ a non-family manager. While this person is ultimately accountable to you, he or she mediates and, if necessary, arbitrates the company's day-to-day problems. In this way, charges of nepotism and family favoritism among non-family staff are nonissues.

As a founder of the family business, you will also want to define and oversee the control factors under which your business operates. You will want to be sure that every employee knows from the start who is in charge of sales, operations, bookkeeping, marketing, advertising, cash flow, etc.; who repairs what; and who reports to whom, when, where, and how. In this way, power squabbles among employees, family and non-family members alike are minimized.

Think through these scenarios at the beginning. They will be different for each family. Plan in advance and establish a chain of authority upon which all family members can agree. When push comes to shove, not everyone may abide by this arrangement, but at least you'll have set a precedent and a frame of reference that can be referred back to when you disagree.

4. Keep all family financial transactions contractual.

It's fine to lend your nephew Jim $100 and take his word that he'll pay you back at the end of the month. But if you lend Jim $85,000 to buy into a business, you'll need more than a handshake if you want to avoid the kind of misunderstandings that end up shattering families.

So be sensible. If you're dealing with a relative on a financial basis, seek a lawyer's help. Get all the details down in a written contract concerning repayment plans, monthly rents, leasing arrangements, interest payments, salaries, benefits, and the like. Don't be casual on this issue.

5. Establish a time line.

Not all family businesses are forever.

Many fifty-plus entrepreneurs intend to invest their money in a hot new business, hire a son or spouse to help run the company, turn a profit, and in ten years put up the business for sale.

Okay. Except that when the day of reckoning comes, your son or spouse may not *want* to sell the business. He or she has a good thing going. The business is keeping the family—*your* family—well fed and happy. Why rock the boat?

Solution: If you want your new business to be time-limited, make this fact clear to all family employees in the early stages. Explain to one and all how you'll be structuring the company, how the proposed time line will work, and when and how you intend to sell or retool or divest yourself of the company's assets.

Again, placing all issues on the table at the beginning can save you a large number of headaches and heartaches at the end.

6. Set up good lines of communication.
It's important that people's problems, suggestions, and gripes be heard. This is especially true of a family business, where unaddressed frustrations can morph into personal family feuds, causing hurt feelings, shouting matches, and even divorces.

So think preventively. Be sure all family members' voices are heard. Keep the channels of communication open. Don't ignore problems, don't let disagreements fester, and don't allow small issues to mushroom into large ones.

It's a good idea, for example, to organize a family-only business meeting once or twice a month. At this family sit-down, all business problems and personal issues are aired and all suggestions heard. Grievances can be ironed out at this time, changes in business policy discussed, and personal conflicts addressed.

Not every meeting will solve every problem, needless to say. But the very fact that you schedule these meetings sends a message to family employees that they are an integral part of the organization. Even if you have only one or two family members working for you, these meetings can go a long way toward defusing potential—or de facto—conflicts.

The question of succession
Somewhere down the line, you will either want to cash out of your new entrepreneurial enterprise, or pass the torch to one of your relatives, presumably one who already works in the business.

If you choose to take the latter route, it's a good idea to start the wheels of succession turning early.

In their standard business school textbook, *Small Business Management*, Justin Longenecker, Carlos Moore, and J. William Petty present a section on family businesses subtitled "Stages in the Process of Succession." According to the authors, succession in a family operation often requires a long process of preparation and transition that unfolds in a series of distinct stages:

1. **Prebusiness stage**—In many cases the successor-to-be learns the family business as a child or teenager. He or she goes to the office or store everyday with Mom and/or Dad, plays with the equipment, makes friends with the employees, and unconsciously absorbs the company's atmosphere and operations. The deep sense of familiarity that results paves the way for this person to become a strong asset to the business later on, and to rank as a logical candidate for succession.
2. **Introductory stages**—Young family members work in the business part-time, during vacations or after school. Here they meet other workers, perform a number of basic jobs, and receive a ground-up education in the daily running of the business.
3. **Functional and advanced functional stages**—After completing their formal education, or after finishing a term of duty in the military, many young people join the family business as full-time employees. They often start at the bottom, carrying boxes in the warehouse, cold calling on the phone, performing janitorial work, making deliveries, or accompanying technicians on service calls. While performing these duties, they gain valuable experience in many different branches of the business. Gradually, they work their way up to full managerial positions.
4. **Early and mature succession**—Eventually, the family employee becomes the de facto or de jure head of the family business. He or she, along with the founder, oversees all supervisory duties, directs employees, and participates in policy decisions. During this time, the successor is intentionally groomed to take over the operation.

In the case of a later-life new career, not all of these stages apply, but many still do. If you are a fifty-plus entrepreneur, keep in mind that in times of transition many family businesses founder and fail, both for financial reasons and personal ones. The remedy is to be proactive, and to set the succession machinery in place from the start. The following procedures will help:

- Establish the plans for your succession at least a year, and preferably several years, before you intend to retire. Doing this helps you avoid the inevitable power struggles that occur among family survivors if you suddenly become disabled, mentally incapacitated (as with a stroke), or die without warning. It is also good business to let everyone know in advance how the succession will work, and who will do what, when, and how, when your retirement time comes.
- Make sure that your successor is adequately prepared to take over the business. Before you step down, encourage successors to participate in running the company and in making key decisions. As your retirement approaches, increase their power and authority. Let them do the important work with clients and business associates. Encourage them to get involved in all aspects of the operation. Ideally, when the time comes for takeover, they will already be partly running the company.
- Be crystal clear when naming your successor. Simply transferring shares of your business to a family group and letting them figure it out from there is a recipe for family war. Far better to provide each key person involved in the transition, family and non-family alike, with a written succession plan. Be sure that all principals read and understand this document.
- Before retirement, schedule a series of meetings with family-company officials. At these meetings, name your successor, discuss the mechanics of the takeover, and describe in detail how the succession plan will work. Holding such formal meetings now will help prevent family members from insisting that they were surprised or blind-sided by your transition policies later on.
- When more than one relative is being groomed to take over your business, be sure there are two ways to do this. The first is with a legal family partnership in which each relative is made a full partner. Though far from ideal, this method is preferable if successors are uncomfortable naming one of themselves as boss. Second is by establishing a "first among equals" plan in which one of the successors oversees the day-to-day running of the company. When major business decisions are made, however, all the partners cast their vote as equals.

- Provide your successor with a clear business plan. Part of this plan will already be in your successor's mental data bank from long experience with the family company. More tangibly, you might draw up a business plan and walk through it with your successor until it becomes second nature. Successors may, of course, diverge from this plan as soon as they take over, heading off in their own directions, but it never hurts to leave a clear instruction manual for a new regime.
- Establish a timetable for your succession. Let involved family members know exactly how long you intend to keep working, when you plan to transfer shares of the company, when you intend to retire, and how long after succession you intend to remain with the company in an advisory or voting capacity (if at all). By keeping key family players informed of your plans in advance, there is little room for accusations and misunderstandings down the line.
- Keep your succession plan flexible. Since the business world is always in flux, and family members' lives change as the years pass, it's best to periodically review your succession plans, and to add modifications when appropriate. Most of all, avoid the "file it and forget it" approach. Life is full of surprises.
- Educate yourself. Read books on family succession. Check out family business-oriented websites. Talk to people with experience. Learn the legal and psychological ins and outs. Here are several excellent books that will get you started:
  - *Family Business Succession*, C. Arnoff, S. McClure, J. Ward
  - *Strategic Planning for the Family Business*, Randel Carlock
  - *Keep the Family Baggage Out of the Family Business*, Quentin Fleming
  - *Getting Along in Family Business*, Edwin Hoover
  - *Family Wealth: Keeping it in the Family*, J. Hughes

Helpful websites include:
- *www.familybusinessmagazine.com*
- *www.ffi.org* (Family Firm Institute, Inc. The International Body for Family Business Professionals)
- *www.family-business-experts.com*

Chapter 9
Why Build When You Can Purchase? The Ins and Outs of Buying an Existing Business

Own your own, on your own

At fifty-six years of age, Jim Lorenzen had more than thirty years' experience under his belt in the field of radio. He had worked on the air and been a salesman, an announcer, a sales manager, and the general manager of a large station. He was familiar with all radio formats, including sports, news, and talk, and he had an A-1 reputation in the industry as an all-around expert.

He was also fed up.

"These big radio companies don't care anything about their employees," Jim told us at a late-night interview session. "I was sick and tired of working for this big station here, that big station there, and then you suddenly see it sold into the next leveraged buyout led by some big Wall Street firm that doesn't know AM from FM! Listen, I eat, sleep, and breathe radio; but the cold, big-business aspect of it was really wearing me down."

During the 1990s, as Jim explained to us, radio went through a major consolidation. Washington removed ownership caps that had existed since the 1930s, and companies that once owned a dozen or so stations now started acquiring hundreds and even thousands of them across the country.

The first thing many of these large companies did when they acquired a network of stations was to set up a single broadcasting studio that piped out uniform programming across the country to each of its satellite stations. People in Bangor, Maine, would now be listening to the exact same talk shows and sports scores as people in Seattle, Washington. As a result of this one-size-fits-all system, the local character of radio stations began to suffer, and longtime listeners drifted away. Soon, many advertisers followed.

But while these mega-broadcasters paid huge prices to build their empires, they didn't always get the results they'd hoped for. Advertising and profits dropped, and after a while, these companies began to sell off their smaller stations at bargain prices.

"This was just the news I had been waiting to hear," Jim told us. "I'd always wanted to own my own radio station. Now the time was right and the opportunity was here."

In 2002, Jim took the leap. Partnering with Tom Klein, his previous boss and a knowledgeable radio veteran, the two men decided to buy up radio stations from the big guys, and run them the way *they* felt stations should be run.

After prolonged negotiations, Jim and Tom purchased several stations from Clear Channel and other companies at half the price these companies had paid for them a few years earlier. These stations needed plenty of TLC, but Jim and Tom knew just what to do to fix them: Give them back their local identity.

They accomplished this task primarily by broadcasting more local news, more local sports, more local talk, and by making sure the music they played appealed to local tastes. They also stressed sales and service in their newly acquired stations, and hired people with real experience in radio. In time, they built strong teams that were committed to their stations and to the communities they served.

Jim and Tom now own seven radio stations throughout the state of Ohio. The recession that began in 2008 has been rough on radio in general, with revenues of big broadcasters slipping by as much as forty percent. But the local nature of Jim and Tom's stations, along with its loyal listenership and sound management policies, has allowed them to make small but steady profits. "When things get better with the economy," Jim said, "they'll get even better with us!"

Jim and Tom's story shows the supreme importance of timing. A few years before their partnership was launched, prices for radio stations were prohibitive. When the big networks started losing money, though, the opportunity was there, and they seized it.

"We bought when the time was right," Jim told us. "But frankly, if we'd waited a few more years, until the recession, we'd have picked up our stations at an even cheaper price. With this economic dip, costs for businesses in general have fallen way below their previous levels. This has been devastating for lots of people, of course. But it has a silver lining, namely, it provides once-in-a-lifetime opportunities for buying an existing business at a bargain-basement price."

Yet even with the right timing, an ongoing business can be lots of trouble if you don't know exactly what you're doing on all business fronts.

Warren and Izzy had been partners in a marketing consulting business for more than twenty-five years. Together they designed ad campaigns for hundreds of companies, from car dealerships to furniture refinishers.

Both men loved developing slogans and brands; writing ad copy; and producing radio, television, and newspaper ads. But as they each neared age sixty, they began to tire of the pressure. How much better it would be, they agreed, to work at a business that was less time-consuming, less pressured, and that involved fewer days on the road.

Since Warren and Izzy lived in Florida, they began talking to local business brokers about purchasing a preexisting business. Working with a price range between $300,000 to $500,000, they looked at health clubs, bowling allies, delis, dry cleaners, bookstores, even a shooting range, and rejected them all. The hours were too long, the business didn't interest them, the location wasn't right—there was always a problem.

Then one day they received a call from an agent about a detailing business.

Detailing is an ultraprecise method for cleaning and restoring automobiles, boats, private planes, and trucks. Even engines, trunks, the inside the glove compartments come out looking factory-fresh when detailers go to work on them. In return for the service, customers pay from $100 to detail a car to more than a thousand dollars for a yacht or a plane.

Warren and Izzy had zero experience in the detailing business, though Warren was a fanatic about keeping his own vehicles clean. The two men believed, however, that their combined business acumen and experience could make this new business work. Both had been managers and supervisors during their careers, and both were expert at supervising and motivating staff.

The detailing company that Warren and Izzy were interested in—we'll call it Super-Finicky Vehicles—seemed to be a highly profitable operation. Their main selling hook was that they provided door-to-door detailing service in the customer's driveway. "No need to come to us—we'll come to you." The company already had a cleaning contract with a local school bus company, plus several contracts for detailing yachts.

At the first meeting with the owners of Super-Finicky, a man and his wife, Warren and Izzy were informed that Super-Finicky had approximately $1.5 million in revenue and $500,000 in profits. The owners would sell them the business for $500,000, payable at closing, plus a note for another $500,000, payable over the next four years.

Fair enough, they thought. Warren and Izzy briefly reviewed the company's records, interviewed a few key employees, and were happy with their findings. Several friends recommended that they hire a lawyer and an accountant to go over the company's books with a fine-tooth comb just to be sure. But Warren and Izzy liked the business, thought their knowledge of finance was sufficient, and without further research, they made a deal.

Big mistake.

Super-Finicky, it turned out, was indeed a functioning business with bona fide customers. It just didn't have as *many* customers as the ex-owners claimed.

Three weeks into their new careers, Warren and Izzy learned that their biggest contract—it was with a bus company and constituted almost half the company's income—had been cancelled weeks before they bought the company. Next, they discovered that Super-Finicky's vehicles were rented, not owned, contrary to what the ex-owners had told them. Worst by far, many of the entries in the Super-Finicky accounting records were faked. The owner of Super-Finicky *and* his wife were crooks—real-life crooks with equally real criminal records, as it turned out. Warren and Izzy referred to them as Bonnie and Clyde.

Warren and Izzy's dream business now turned into an ongoing lawsuit. The dishonest owners moved to the other side of the country, pursued by Warren and Izzy's lawyer at significant expense and aggravation. As of the writing of this book, nothing has been resolved, and the case drags on.

Warren and Izzy may someday negotiate a financial settlement, but it is unlikely. Meanwhile, they were forced to close Super-Finicky and are now back at work as marketing consultants.

Oh, and they lost all their investment as well.

Moral: Do your research, avoid businesses that you know nothing about, work with professionals to review a company's records, and be ever vigilant.

The pluses of buying an existing business

Jim's and Warren and Izzy's stories show that like any other business venture, buying an existing business can be a positive or negative experience. We want yours to be a positive one. Here are some plusses and minuses to be aware of. First, the plusses:

- **Buying an existing business saves time**—Why spend years building a business from scratch when you can purchase one that's already standing and turning a profit?
- **Buying an existing business eliminates some risks**—Building a new business is perilous. You can make mistakes. Undercapitalization, hidden startup costs, picking the wrong location, hiring the wrong employees, selling the wrong products can all bring a new business to its knees. When you purchase an ongoing business, you don't worry about these things.
- **Buying an existing business *may* save you money**—In some cases, perhaps many cases, it is cheaper to buy an existing business than to build a similar one from scratch.
- **Buying an existing business gets you to the fun part more quickly**—You may prefer running a business, working with customers, supervising employees, and, of course, making money to renting space, ordering stationery, and other drudgework associated with a startup.

Then there are the minuses:
- **Buying an ongoing business can be expensive**—You may not have to think about startup costs, but with an ongoing business, the asking price includes time and labor already been put in, plus name, reputation, and proven profit-making performance. Buying an ongoing business may also require the payment of a sizeable amount of money all at once.
- **There are always risks**—As in the tale of Warren and Izzy, what you see is not always what you get. Even if you buy the business from basically honest sellers, they may still not be completely candid about potential problems. Also, established customers may bolt if ownership changes.
- **You may have to compromise**—Finding *exactly* the right business is tough. For example, instead of buying a quilting supply store, you may have to purchase a crafts supply store that sells quilt-making materials, but requires you to focus on more than just quilts.
- **Searching for a viable existing business takes time and energy**—It may indeed save you time to buy rather than build. But searching for the right business and negotiating a deal that works for you can eat into your day.

Buying an existing business in a downturned economy

In turmoil there is opportunity—and risk.

The major recession that began in 2008 reduced consumer spending, slashed bank lending, crippled the real estate industry, and hobbled some of the bedrock businesses of the world economy.

That's the good news.

At least it is *possibly* the good news for you as the prospective buyer of an existing business because all of these factors make a business worth less than it had been pre-2008, and thus make it cheaper for you to buy. That's the opportunity side of the equation.

There is a risk side during down economic times as well, though.

Such a volatile environment makes it difficult, if not impossible, to make sales projections. If you intend to purchase a jewelry store that earned $1.3 million in sales in 2007, and then $845,000 in 2008 because of a dismal holiday season, how do you estimate what sales will be in 2010?

The simple truth is that no one knows. You can make a case for just about any number.

For example, you can be pessimistic and assume the business will continue to decline because of a weak economy and consumer reluctance to spend, or you can be more optimistic and say that, like most recessions, it will last two, two-and-a-half years at most, and then get back on a growth track.

No one knows. Uncertainty about the economy is a risk you take at any time, but it is especially prevalent during a recession.

Throughout this book, we have emphasized the fact that there are certain proven ways to manage and control risk. These strategies are effective during any economic climate, but they are crucial if there is a strong probability that the economic climate will continue to downslide. Here are some of these strategies again for consideration as you search for a business and negotiate its purchase:

- **Pay for the business over time**—Sellers of businesses typically prefer to be paid all at once, but in hard times, you can usually negotiate a deal that includes some payment at closing and the balance paid over time. The balance can even be pegged to the performance of the business. This is called an "earn-out." As the business makes money for you, the seller receives a share of sales or profits. Different times require different tactics.
- **Don't assume all the current owner's obligations**—He or she may have a lease, contracts with suppliers, or advertising contacts. You can make renegotiating these contracts a condition for buying the business. When the owner views negotiating a new deal as preferable to seeing the business fold, you have achieved your point of highest leverage. Use it.
- **If you are ready to buy a business, think positively to yourself, but base your negotiations with the seller on the fact that times are hard**—That is, let it be known that you believe the economy will continue to head south, and negotiate from this standpoint. Assume that the seller is anxious to make a deal and will be willing to meet you

more than halfway. If it turns out that your pessimism is unwarranted, you will have nonetheless paid a lower price, perhaps, or have spaced your payments over time and to your advantage, or you may even have renegotiated contracts or leases for lower rates. And if the economy continues to falter or the business hits other problems, you will have more time to meet your goals.

How to buy an existing business

Buying an existing business starts with due diligence, the process of collecting all relevant documents and thoroughly researching the business. A lawyer or accountant—or both—who specialize(s) in this field will be helpful.

Here is an overview of what you need:

Financial records for the past five years.

- **Financial statements**—Such as income statements and balance sheets.
- **Tax returns**—For state, local, and federal taxes, including information about any tax liens, audits, or reviews.
- **Details of accounts receivable**—To tell you which parties owe the business money. By seeing how many of these accounts take an inordinately long period of time to pay—or how many do not pay at all—can help you make a ballpark estimate of how many delinquent accounts you can expect.
- **Details of accounts payable**—To tell you how much money the business owes its suppliers, employees, and landlord. If the business is very slow in paying its bills, it may be struggling with cash flow. As a result, you, as the new owner, may have considerable bad will to overcome with these important business partners. Be warned, and bring up this fact in your negotiations.
- **Inventory**—If you are buying a business such as a hardware supplier or bookstore that requires significant inventory, you need a precise accounting of what stock is available. One way that sellers take advantage of buyers is to let the inventory levels drop to minimum just prior to selling the business. This sneaky bit of sleight-of-hand saves them money and

forces the buyer to spend more than anticipated to replenish inventory. Again, be on the alert.

Contracts and other documents.
- **Contracts**—These include leases; contracts with customers, vendors, suppliers and unions; and shareholder agreements.
- **Organizational documents**—If you and your lawyer have decided to structure the purchase by buying the company stock, you will need to see the current owner's articles of incorporation, bylaws, and minutes of board and shareholder meetings. Most business purchases are structured as asset purchases, meaning that you buy the assets used in running the business, such as its name, inventory, and contracts, but not its actual legal entity such as an S Corporation.
- **Litigation and other legal issues**—If the business has been sued, threatened with a lawsuit, or has disputes outstanding, you need to know all about them.
- **Employment contracts**—Employees may have contracts that obligate a new owner to meet certain salary levels or provide termination benefits. They may also have noncompete clauses in their contracts to prevent them from going to work for your competition.

Asset information.
- **Real estate**—If you are purchasing a building or land, you will need a full description of the property, plus a record of any inspections and violations, a description of the applicable zoning, and possibly an environmental report.
- **Intellectual property**—Patents, trade secrets, trademarks, service marks, and copyrights are the most important assets for many businesses, and these must be fully disclosed and legally transferred to you. Such properties can include less obvious items such as logo designs or proprietary scientific knowledge. All must be researched and identified during your due diligence.
- **Licenses and permits**—Many businesses, from television stations to hot dog stands, require government licenses or permits to operate, and these must be reviewed.

Customer information.
- **Customer lists and profiles**—As well as the business itself, you are also purchasing the relationships the business maintains with its customers. You need to know who these customers are, how much they spend, and what they like to buy. Current owners may make sales calls on key accounts, or they may send holiday cards to a contact list. Building and retaining strong customer relationships is at the center of any business. Find out as much as you can about this client base ahead of time.
- **Problems and disputes**—Identify all potential problems such as disputes, returns, and recent changes in buying patterns that might reflect the end of the relationship with a particular customer or segment of customers.

Marketing information.
- **Marketing efforts**—You need to know about any recent marketing efforts and their effectiveness. These efforts may include trade show booths, direct mail campaigns, and advertising in traditional media or through the Internet.

GO FORTH AND PROSPER!

The Second Chance Revolution is real. It is happening today and it is growing. You are a part of it. People over fifty have the skills and experience to create and grow businesses. Being an entrepreneur offers a way to achieve satisfaction with work and to provide needed financial support. We hope this book will help you successfully along this path by alerting you to opportunities, giving you a roadmap, and teaching you strategies to minimize the risk that is a part of every business venture.

We hope you will share your stories and experiences with us and your fellow fifty-plus entrepreneurs at our website *www.secondchancerevolution.com* or *www.taketwoevent.com*.

Index

7-Eleven, 131

AARP, 5–6, 38, 51–2, 104–5
accountants, 33, 42, 54, 61, 69, 76, 82–4, 89, 113, 147, 149–50, 152, 162, 172, 176
age-related bias, 20
ageism, 8, 20
Ali, Muhammad, 73
Amabile, Teresa M., 26
American Association of Franchisees and Dealers (AAFD), 142
American Marketing Association (AMA), 142
amortization, 67
angel investors, 21, 54, 61–2, 64
antidiscrimination laws, 90
Apple Computer, 37
appliance repair, 33
Arnoff, Craig, 167
Asia Dispensing Company, 123
asset-based valuation, 66
Astor, Brooke, 92
astrologer, 33
AT&T Small Business Lending Corporation, 148
auto insurance, 87

Bahadur, Ram, vi, 109–10

Bankable Business Plans for Entrepreneurial Ventures, 108
Bankable Business Plans, 2nd Edition, 108
banks, 21, 36, 53–8, 63–5, 69–72, 114, 119, 135, 148, 174
Baruch College, City University of New York, v–vi, 1–2, 60, 127
bed-and-breakfast, 10, 161
beekeeper, 33
beginning entrepreneurs, 13–23, 25–52
benefits, 6, 26, 81
Blank, Arthur, 37
board of advisors, 77–9
board of directors, 61, 74–5, 77–9, 84, 87–8, 162
Bond's Franchise Guide, 143
boomers, vii–viii, 3–8, 21
borrower, 54, 57, 64, 69–70
broadcasting, 169–71
building a board of advisors or directors, 77–9
Burger King, 134
business insurance, 87–8, 110–11, 114
business plan, 14, 18, 21, 23, 38–9, 54–6, 58, 66–9, 77, 79–80, 107–9, 136, 147–9, 152, 161–2, 167
business-interruption insurance, 88
buying an existing business, 169–78

C corporation, 84–5
Campbell, Joseph, 25–6
career selection, 27–37, 42–3
Caring Transitions, 146
Carlock, Randel, 167
cash flow/EBITDA based, 67
CDC/504 loan program, 148
Census Bureau, 50
Chambliss, Jim, 39
character loan, 69–70
Chrysler, 11
Claritas, 50
Clear Channel, 170
clown, 33
collateral, 57–60, 63, 69–72
Commerce Clearing House (CCH), 68
computer repair service, 33
consultant, 33, 35
contracts, 57–8, 129–30, 138, 149, 163, 177
corporate investments, 62–3
costs of living, 6
credit card, 54, 59, 69
credit history, 53, 69
credit report, 71
credit scoring, 71–2
CUNY Baruch College, v–vii, 1–2, 60, 127

DBA or doing-business-as name, 89
debt, 57–9
Delafield, Wisconsin, 56
Deleuze, Robert, 74–6, 79
depreciation, 67, 115
desktop publisher, 33
direct investments, 62–3
directors, 61, 74–5, 77–9, 84, 87–8, 162
directors and officers liability, 77, 87–8
directors insurance, 77, 87–8
disability insurance, 88
discounted cash flow, 66
Domino's Pizza, 131
downsized, 9, 37
Dunkin' Donuts, 131, 132
Dylan, Bob, 5

EBITDA, 67
Eisenhower, Dwight D., 5

employment contracts, 177
entrepreneurial opportunities, 41–2
entrepreneurial professions, 25–52
equity funding, 57–8
estimating your company's value, 65–7
exit strategies, 58, 62, 155
extrinsic motivation, 26
Eye Candy Eyewear, 56
eyeglass business, 55–6, 63

Facebook.com, 120–1
Fair, Isaac, and Company (FICO), 71
family, 21, 52, 54, 60–1, 65, 115–6, 120, 148, 154–5
family business, 21, 34, 154–5, 157–67
Family Business Succession, 167
Family Firm Institute, Inc., 167
family goals, 44–5
Family Wealth: Keeping it in the Family, 167
Family-Business-Experts.com, 167
FamilyBusinessMagazine.com, 167
Field, Lawrence N., v
financial goals, 44–5
financial models, 67–9
financial records, 132, 147, 176–7
Fleming, Quentin, 167
flower shop, 37–8
Foodtopia, 74–6, 80
Ford, Henry, 81
Franchise Opportunities Guide, 143
Franchise.org, 38, 143
franchises, 127–55
FranchiseTimes.com, 142
FranNet, 142
Freud, Sigmund, 6–7
friends, 54, 60–1, 65, 120
furniture maker, 33

G.E. Financial, 148
general liability, 87
general partnerships, 83, 85
Getting Along in Family Business, 167
Goethe, Johann Wolfgang von, 18
going public, 54, 64–5
Gooden, Joseph, vi, 10
government loan guarantees, 70
grant writer, 33

Grateful Dead, 127

Handyman Matters, 139–41
Harper's Bazaar, 92
Harvard University, 26
health benefits, 80–1, 88, 158
health care costs, 6
health insurance, 86–7
home crafts, 33
Home Depot, 37
home manicure service, 33
home office environment, 111–13, 115–16
home office tax deduction, 113–15
home-business, 91–116
home-business cons, 101–5
Homes, Anne, vi
Hoover, Edwin, 167
Hornbeck, Paula, vi, 55–8, 63
Hughes, James, 167

Idea Development Grid, 47–50
illustrator, 33
immigration rules, 89
inflation, 6
inspections, 89, 132, 177
insurance, 74–5, 110–11. *See also specific types of insurance.*
insurance benefits, 86–7
intellectual property, 177
InterContinental Hotels Group, 131
Internal Revenue Service (IRS), 73, 83, 89, 113–15
International Franchise Association (IFA), 38, 142–3
Internet boom, 18
intrinsic motivation, 26
investor considerations, 85

Jacobs, Sarah Martha, 12
Jobs, Steve, 37

Kagan, Robert, 16
Kauffman Foundation, viii, 21, 38
Kay, Mary, 36–7
KCSourceLink, 38
Keep the Family Baggage Out of the Family Business, 175

Kentucky Fried Chicken, 131, 132
KFC Corp., 131, 132
Kingston Trio, 127
Klein, Tom, vi, 170
Krasner, Leslie, vi, 42
Kroc, Ray, 10–11

Lahey, Lisa L., 16
Lamie, John, vi, 121–3
lawn care service, 33
Lawrence N. Field Center for Entrepreneurship, 2, 12, 109
lawyers, 54, 58, 61–2, 82–4, 107, 143, 149, 162–3, 176–7
legal issues, 98, 177
lenders, 54–5, 57–8, 63–4, 66, 69–72, 77, 88, 108, 148–9
liability considerations, 84
licenses, 88, 98, 115, 177
life insurance, 88
lifestyle goals, 44–5
limited liability companies, 84
limited liability partnerships and professional corporations, 84
limited partnerships, 83–4
lines of communication, 164
lines of credit, 54, 57–9
LinkedIn.com, 120–1
liquidation value, 66–7
litigation, 160, 177
loans, 53–9, 63–4, 67, 69–72, 135–6, 144, 148
Longenecker, Justin, 164
Lorenzen, Jim, 169

MacDonald brothers, 10–11
MacDonald, Dick, 10–11
MacDonald, Mac, 10–11
mail order company, 10, 33, 102
Martens & Heads!, 119
Martens, Maxine, vi, 118–9
Mary Kay Cosmetics, 36, 37
McClure, Stephen, 167
McDonald's, 11, 76, 130, 131, 136
McKelvey, Andrew J., 37
medical benefits, 80–1, 88, 158
medical savings account, 86
Medicare, 86, 87, 89

microbrewery, 37
Mid-America Minority Business Development Council, 38
Milwaukee, 55–6
Monster.com, 37
Moody, Harry R., vii–viii
Moore, Carlos, 164
MOOT Corp., 164
mortgages, 9, 54, 57, 70
MyFico.com, 71

networking, 117–26, 151–2
networks, 110, 120–3, 151–2
newsletter writer, 33

occupational safety and health administration (OSHA) rules, 89–90
officers, 77, 87–8, 143
officers insurance, 11
options for legal structure, 82–5
organizational documents, 177
Other People's Money (OPM), 60
outsourcing, 20, 81–2

Pacheco, Louise, 98
part-time work, 34, 60, 99, 111
Payne, Bill, 21
payroll taxes, 14, 89
pensions, 6, 9, 20, 44, 62, 81
permits, 88–90, 98, 115, 177
permits and licenses, 88, 98, 115, 177
personal goals, 150–1
personal guarantee, 53, 56, 58, 63, 70, 71
Petty, J. William, 164
photographer, 33
Pizza Hut, 131
Plaxo.com, 121
professional growth goals, 44
property and casualty, 87

QuickBooks, 14
Quiznos, 133

radio, 169–71
radio stations, 170
RE/MAX, 131
real estate, 57, 66–7, 177
registering your name, 89

replacement value, 66
research, 31, 50, 106–7, 39–44, 176–7
retirement, 3–8, 14, 16, 20, 166
revenue-or profit-based valuation, 67
risk, 16–17, 35–6, 59, 63, 69, 122, 150–1, 174–5
Rockefeller, John D., 41
Rolling Stone Magazine, 5
rubber stamp business, 33

S corporation, 83, 85, 177
SatisfactionMag.com, 39
SCAMPER technique, 29–30
seamstress, 33
secured debt, 57–8
self-employment, vii–viii, 8–23, 25–52
Service Corps of Retired Executives (SCORE), 38
sexual harassment laws, 90
shareholder, 57, 83–5, 177
shareholder's agreement, 58, 177
Skates, Darrel, vi, 98
skills, 15–6, 37–41, 44–6, 50–2, 116, 134, 141, 153
Small Business Administration, 19, 39, 52, 62, 70–1, 109, 135–6, 148, 150
Small Business Administration 7(a) loan, 135–6, 148
Small Business Management, 164
social goals, 44–5
sole proprietorships, 83, 85
Sonic Drive-In Restaurants, 131
Starcusso, Jeffrey, 11
state and local taxes, 89
Strand Bookstore, 92
Strategic Planning for the Family Business, 167
Subway, 131
succession, 164–7
Super-Finicky Vehicles, 172–3
supply chain management, 82

tax accountant, 33
tax considerations, 84
taxes, 67, 83–6, 88–9, 113–5, 154, 176
technology, 19, 116, 153
technology skills, 153
The Money Store, 148

The New Yorker, 10
Thometz, Kurt, vi, 92, 95
Toffler, Alvin, 6
Trafford, Abigail, 7
translator, 33
tutor, 33, 36
Twitter.com, 121

U.S. Franchise News, 142
umbrella policies, 88
upholsterer, 33
using lawyers and accountants, 82–4

Venture Assessment Tool (VAT), 43–52
venture capital, 54, 62, 65
VocationVacations.com, 43
Vreeland, Diana, 92

Ward, John, 167
Wayne, Gene, vi, 139–41
website designer, 33
Winter, Alan, vi, 145–6
worker's compensation, 87
worksheet for building a board of
　　directors or advisors, 78–9
WorldFranchising.com, 143
Wozniak, Steve, 137
writer, 33

Zach, Martha, vi, 10